WHAT'S WRONG WITH

WRONG WITH

U̶S̶, U̶.S̶., U.$?

Howard Bobb

authorHOUSE®

AuthorHouse™
1663 Liberty Drive
Bloomington, IN 47403
www.authorhouse.com
Phone: 1-800-839-8640

First published by AuthorHouse 11/2/2009

ISBN: 978-1-4389-7843-7 (e)
ISBN: 978-1-4389-7842-0 (sc)
ISBN: 978-1-4389-7841-3 (hc)

Printed in the United States of America
Bloomington, Indiana

This book is printed on acid-free paper.

TABLE OF CONTENTS

FOREWORD

I am a conservative, somewhat republican. I voted for Barry Goldwater, Richard Nixon and most of the rest. I vote for what the republican party is supposed to stand for, but in many cases does not. I am basically a frugal man who likes to take care of myself. I have taught myself to do home repairs and remodeling, I have worked on cars and even once built a kit car. I mow my own grass and paint my own home. I went straight from high school into the Navy. After my discharge I worked for one year at two jobs until I was hired by the Philadelphia Police Department.

During twenty three years in the Police Department, I was promoted four times. I went to night school for fifteen years and received a Bachelors, Masters and Law Degree. After the Police Department I practiced law for twenty five years. I have never been an insider, but I believe I know what is going on and I don't like it.

I am proud of my Police career and feel that during that time I kept my balance by remembering always that I worked for the people I policed and not for the Police Department. The Police Department has no earnings. There is no product to sell and no profit to be made. When I received my check every two weeks it was because taxpayers worked and the government took some of their money to provide protection. I tried to give the people their money's worth.

Many people see the same things that I see every day and perhaps don't get the same meaning from the events. I am not critical of them. I just feel that they are not noticing the same things that I notice.

Like everyone else who tries to write a book about something, I feel that I have a message to send out to anyone who would read my words. It is my hope that my words might lead people to look at events and what we have become as Americans in a different way. Perhaps I can lead readers to recognize the values of our forefathers and try to bring those values back into our twenty-first century life. In the twenty-first century we see a world that is shrunken in size and time. A pioneer's trip from the East coast to California may have taken weeks or months and been fraught with hardship. Today the trip takes six hours or so, and you can lean back in the seat with a beverage of your choice. At the same time our private lives have shrunk. Fraternal organizations are dying from lack of membership. Community is a place where you live, a location, but it is not a part of your life. Even local taverns have become sports bars, where conversation is difficult and your attention is grabbed by the multitude of televisions playing everywhere.

We don't ponder anymore. There is no time. We have our day mapped out on the blackberry and we cannot deviate or the whole schedule will go to hell in a hand basket. We need to ponder. Ponder why your congressman and senator is an elitist that you cannot get to talk to unless it is election time and he wants to talk to you and all your friends. Ponder why the congressman and senator are your employee and you cannot get to see or talk to them. I have pondered these and many other things and have concluded that one person cannot solve the problems of our society and our world. The solution lies within the grasp of the populace. The populace can solve a problem simply by recognizing that it is a problem. Once it is recognized the search will begin. Many will come forth with potential solutions. The populace will decide which solution is best. The best solutions will be determined by common sense. I have tried to make common sense a part of my life. I think that many people have relied on others to make decisions for them. It hasn't worked out too well in my opinion, and I think it is time that we begin to look at our problems and demand solutions from ourselves and others. Politicians and the media are failing us, and we are mistaken to relinquish the power of decision to them.

I hope that you will enjoy this book and that you will ponder the meaning of my writing.

GREED

Greed is defined as avarice, which is defined as excessive or insatiable desire for wealth or gain, cupidity, which is further defined as inordinate desire for wealth. Excessive, insatiable and inordinate desire for wealth describes the error in the thought process of the overwhelming majority of the folks who live in these United States. It is at the core of what's wrong with us.

Having great wealth and fame are sought after as a means of bringing satisfaction and happiness to the individual. However, most individuals lack the common sense to examine this premise to see if it is really true. If you were to ask people the amount of money that they would like or need to have, most would have trouble coming up with a number that meant anything to them. A thorough questioning of individual respondents would lead to the result that most would not have put much thought into the actual amount of money that they would need to provide themselves with the lifestyle they would like to lead. Nor would they have a reasonable explanation for the desire to lead that specific lifestyle. A recent poll of young people supported this conclusion when a majority indicated that their great wish was to be famous. Rich and famous seems to be an end unto itself.

The fallacy of this thinking is that being rich has a great number of pitfalls. For example, how would you know which of your friends really cared about you and which wanted to be around you simply because you had wealth? Would people who associated with you resent you for your wealth? They could perhaps feel that you didn't deserve the wealth. Maybe they would be unable to recognize the superior talent which enabled you to attain wealth. Would people question your values when you purchased something that was on sale or not the top of the line? Would you engage in conspicuous consumption or would you purchase things you really wanted or needed? Would you ever feel safe or would you envy the regular person with the anonymity to not feel threatened by those who might try to punish you for your wealth or profit by exploiting your wealth and fame?

The wish for fame, as stated by the people in the poll, does not include the desire to be acknowledged for accomplishment, just fame. What has brought about this unthinking and poorly constructed aim? For the most part, it is the media. Recently Paris Hilton went to jail. If she had been just a regular person, who had violated her probation, no one would have known or cared. (Except perhaps for her friends and family). However, this event was on the National and International News. When she was released it was a coup to have her on a talk show to discuss her imprisonment, as short as it was. Why is she a celebrity and why is she in demand? The media creates the demand by the manner in which they present a celebrity. Celebrity is defined as; the state of being celebrated; a celebrated person. Take notice that in that definition, there is no specific accomplishment indicating the reason for the celebration. We all know that Paris Hilton is rich. We also know that she did not create the wealth through her own accomplishment. We know that she is somewhat attractive. She had a short stint on a television show that provided proof that she was not an accomplished actress, or at least did not display that type of accomplishment in the show.

Another thing we know about Paris Hilton is her famous name and family. Her family is the obvious source of the wealth. Among the many things we don't know about her is her level of education. Did she graduate from High School? College? Did she receive honors for her education? Has she ever held a job, except for the television show or being paid for some personal appearance? How about her I.Q.? I would venture that 99% of the people who hang on every word concerning Ms. Hilton could not answer any of the foregoing questions.

So why is she newsworthy? The answer is simply because it is either her or someone else. This is not a castigation of Paris Hilton. It is not intended to single her out. There seems to be an endless list of people just like her or enough like her to fill magazine after magazine with photos and stories of their every slip or embarrassment. All news all the time requires fodder. Fodder is defined as something that is used to supply a constant demand. But simple fodder is not really enough. ABC, NBC, CBS, FOX, CNN, WNBC, and on and on, all require not just fodder, but fodder which is more exciting than the fodder being shown on the competitor's show. When one show is advertising a conversation with a mass murderer on death row, the competition must come up with something better than, "tune in tonight and watch Clyde Fergus's tomatoes grow one millimeter per hour." If Clyde's vegetables are all that they have, they are going to dress up that tomato in a gown and pearls and make you feel as though you are going to miss the advent of a new age of vegetables. If you don't watch you will miss the story which is going to affect the World population by stamping out hunger and disease. It doesn't matter that when you turn it on all you'll see is a tomato. What matters is that you turned on their station and the ratings responded.

Why do they get away with feeding us fodder with steak sauce and a sprig of parsley and making us believe it is gourmet faire? We have too much time on our hands. How can that be true you may ask. Well the long and short of it is that we have become use to labor saving devises. When I was a young boy growing up in Philadelphia, few people had cars. There was no television until I was about nine years old. We rode trolley cars and buses to go places. No one carried a portable radio. We used wringer washing machines and clothes lines to dry our clothes. In the winter or if it was raining, the clothesline was in the basement. Life took time. Preparing a meal took a good part of the afternoon. Cleaning up after the meal meant doing the dishes and putting them away. Laundry took time.

This is not meant to criticize all of the improvements that have occurred during my lifetime. Many diseases have been cured. Today, Consumption is not a word that brings to mind an illness, but in the forties and early fifties it was the wasting away of a person who had

Tuberculosis. No one under the age of seventy knows anyone who had TB. Polio is no more. Dishwashers have eliminated germs passing from family member to family member, primarily because the water temperature is high enough to kill germs. The positive list goes on and on.

But there is a negative side. SPEED is the title of the next chapter, and will be explored as the second largest fault with our world today. But here, speed can be defined as the savior and the enemy. Speed allows us to complete tasks that used to take all day in just a few minutes. The result is not more time for more accomplishment, but the demand that anything and everything we do must be done in the shortest amount of time. Therefore, what we want is someone to think out the story for us and tell us what is really important. As a young boy riding public transportation, I saw trains full of people reading the newspaper. The newspapers had to tell the complete story to compete with the other papers. People who read were looking for the story to bring them something. They want to know what was going on in their world and their neighborhood. They wanted it to make sense and prove the conclusions. Newspaper stories that might have taken fifteen or twenty minutes to read are now condensed into sensational blurbs that are spoken to us with a conclusion that we accept. The conclusion may not be obvious in the tone or the specific information from the story that is presented to us, but it is there none the less.

Most of us today have lost the desire to attain wealth by accomplishment over time. When I was growing up in the fifties and sixties, it was not uncommon for someone to become an apprentice. Not just an apprentice carpenter or plumber, but an apprentice salesman, storekeeper, warehouseman, truck driver, mechanic or any other of many professions. Some would like to restrict the word profession to apply only to those who are educated to become the tradesman in their field such as an accountant , lawyer or a doctor. My view, however, is different.

I was a police officer in Philadelphia for quite a few years and during that time of patrolling the city I saw many job sites. Some were huge construction sites and some small home remodeling or beautification. I watched one such small job of construction being done by two people. One, a laborer and the other a stone mason. The stone mason was of Italian descent. He appeared to be, perhaps forty years of age, and small in height. He had strong hands and arms which I noticed as he worked. I watched him over a period of a week or ten days. I would check the progress of the wall when I went on duty and periodically I would ride by and sometime even select a vantage point from which I could observe his work.

His work consisted of supervising the mixing of mortar cement. Both he and the laborer had a hand in the process. Once mixed, the laborer would continue to tend to the mortar to insure that it remained fresh and well mixed, and would from time to time refill the smaller pan from which the stone mason worked. The mason would pick up a stone from the pile and heft it from side to side, examining the quality of the various views of the stone. He would examine, at the same time the next area in which he would insert the stone. After choosing the appropriate view of the stone to face the world, he would then work the bottom, top, sides and back of the stone with what appeared to be a brick hammer. The hammer had a sharp chisel like blade on one end and a hammer on the other. When he finished shaping the stone the way he wanted it, he placed the stone in a bed of mortar filling all of the gaps between the stones beneath and the ones along side.

Many times he would stand before the wall with a stone and then decide it was not the right place in the wall for that stone and he would put it back on the pile and search for another. When the wall was finished I thought that the man had created a masterpiece. There was balance in the colors and textures of the stones making up the wall. The edges were straight and true and the top was even and in balance with the house behind it. The house became the nicest house on the block. To me then, and today, the stone mason was a professional, an artist whose able hands brought artistry and pleasure. He enhanced the look of a home and brought pride and pleasure to the beneficiary of his work, the homeowner.

I never knew the man before or since. I did not engage him in conversation, but overheard him speaking to the laborer. He spoke with Italian accented English. I never heard him raise his voice or speak in anger. He seemed to be at one with his task. I have no idea what he might have charged to build the wall. Whether wall building was his main profession or a side line, that made him some extra money. I don't know if the customer was satisfied with wall or the price that was paid to the mason. I only know my own feelings toward the man and the job that he did. The man should have been proud of himself and proud of his talent and success.

It would be easy to say I was envious of his skill, but I don't think that explains it. When a professional golfer makes a great shot, a baseball player hit's a homerun, a quarterback throws a touchdown pass, we can think, gee I wish I could do that. We can even think that the person is lucky to have such a skill. But the reality is, for the most part, the person that we watch, has spent many hours, weeks and years learning the trade. The luck is having the physical attributes necessary to perform the task.

The mason may not have been able to run fast. He may not have been able to throw a baseball with accuracy or hit one with a bat. But he had good hands, arms, shoulders and back, which he obviously made stronger through work. He was capable of handling heavy stones with one hand, flipping them from side to side and hitting them just so with his hammer, to shape them perfectly for his growing masterpiece.

Was the mason rich? Probably not. He was, however, an accomplished professional. I am sure that he got many referrals from the job that he completed and could have, from those jobs, made a reasonable amount of money. What is reasonable you might ask? Would that Mason's profit from constructing the wall and his future profits from referrals make him rich and famous? Probably not. But, depending on the Mason's state of mind, the money he made would have been reasonable if it enabled him to provide for his family. If he was respected by his family and neighbors for the talents that he possessed and earned a living from, he might have been happy. If his wife and children were adequately fed and clothed, and he had the funds to save something toward the future, perhaps he would feel that his earnings were reasonable.

Would we find it reasonable today? Would we hold the Mason in high esteem? Probably not. Much of the world of construction has been streamlined eliminating the man-hours of the artisan. Buildings can be constructed to exacting standards and windows and doors are delivered ready to be installed. Brick walls are delivered to the site and installed in a matter of hours. Fascia stone is prefabricated and installed without the need for shaping. These trades have gone the way of the blacksmith. The auto mechanic while not fading into the historic past has had to modify his training. On board computers run the systems of your automobile. The auto mechanic is now called a technician. The technician must read the technical manuals and attach your car to sensing devices that inform the technician what part has to be replaced. No more gapping sparking plugs, setting the timing, gapping the points, adjusting the valves, etc. The computers tell the technician what parts are broken and need replacement. The technician may be held in esteem by the person in need of the service, but it is hard not to realize that the computers are doing the expert work and the technician the grunt work.

Doctors and lawyers are likewise affected. Medically, there are ever more tests to diagnose all of the afflictions that people suffer. Each day there are items in the news that describe the most recent breakthrough and in some cases confusing conclusions. In the fifties (1950s) there were articles concerning the health risks of smoking cigarettes. Over the years these warnings became increasingly severe until now we are informed that people should not be allowed to smoke in the presence of others. The cigarette warnings were the exception. Alcohol consumption was bad and then somewhat good. Red wine is healthy (in moderation). Alcohol (in moderation) at bedtime can be healthy. Caffeine is good and then it's bad. Surgical procedures are also constantly changing. Mastectomy vs. Lumpectomy are debated. Xrays, CTscans, MRIs, etc. have replaced the professional guessing game that doctors engaged in in the fifties. The fifties doctors were trained to listen to patients and question them regarding symptoms. From those answers and limited diagnostic tools, the doctor concluded the diagnosis. Now it is done by machines, computers and science. The doctor is no less skilled, but the patient recognizes that the testing is the defining factor.

Lawyers in olden times went to libraries to research cases and legal principles. Now they have legal research at their fingertips that can answer any inquiry in seconds. Legal research like any other type of research required the person to have knowledge and a good memory. The correct terminology was required to research a legal point. Many hours could be wasted by the novice researcher who could not recognize the area of the law that must be tapped into to find the appropriate caselaw that is on point to the question of the particular case. Now the whole library can be found inside the office computer.

What does it all mean? The need to feel that we are individually accomplished is necessary for all of us. All of our tasks can be modified by modern technology. Having a skill that is replaced by a machine can be damaging to our self esteem. The fact that any task can be replaced in today's world with such blinding speed is daunting. What should we train to be when we grow up? It's hard to say today. My uncle was an electronic and audio wizard. He worked for PHILCO in the developmental laboratory, and worked on developing better speakers, stereo systems, microphones, etc. He was a party to the company obtaining many patents. He also worked on computers in their initial stage. The original hardwired and glasstubed computer was a huge machine that in some installations was on a floor suspended for airflow so that the air conditioner could maintain the machine at a constant temperature. The original computers took up the space of a very large room. I have no expertise in this field, but I would say, without any fear of contradiction, that the room size computer is dwarfed by the capabilities of a hand held computer/phone. Does that make my uncle's accomplishments any less? I think not. I went to my uncle's home and he proudly had me sit in a chair in the center of the living room so that I could hear the orchestra play around me on the stereo. I could hear violins come from one side and trumpets from the other. Every instrument came to my hearing from a different direction. Today we would all say so what. A low priced system purchased in a department store can do the same thing, probably better. No one buying the department store unit would know the contribution of my uncle. My uncle never became rich or famous. However, everyone who knew my uncle respected and admired him. More importantly, my uncle respected and admired himself.

Being rich and famous is fleeting. The money may last, but usually the fame does not. Sometimes the money doesn't either. The obituaries usually list notable people who have passed on. Unless the celebrities pass at an early age, there are few who are individually remembered. How many of us remember the stars in the movie "Gone with the Wind." Even if there are a few of us that remember Clark Gable, what else do we remember about him? He was exceedingly famous at the time the movie released. Did he die rich or poor? I don't know. I do know that the English actor Terry Thomas, who I enjoyed immensely, died without much in the way of money.

Let's ask ourselves a few questions regarding wealth and fame. Of those people that we regard as famous, how many would you feel are happy in their fame? We get to look into the lives of those who do negative things and to a much lesser extent those who do positive things. A local newswoman had an encounter with the Police that cast her in a poor light. She may or may not suffer professionally from her misstep. But, for the moment, she has gotten press ink and broadcasting time that would make a politician envious. Her picture is in the paper, she is talked about on the news and is the subject of talk radio for hours on end. On the other hand, if a local person of moderate fame bought food for a homeless shelter, or bought toys for tots, they might get an honorable mention at the end of the Eleven O'clock News. The next day no one would remember. It should be easy to conclude that it is easier to get noticed for negative behavior than positive. Why therefore would anyone aspire to be famous? Our main view into the lives of the famous is usually through a negative lens. And when it is for something positive, tune in and it will somehow be made negative by the media. The news adage "if it bleeds, it leads," is a truism. Like the chicken and egg question, no one can be sure whether the creation of the truism has been encouraged by the masses, or creates in the masses a level of excitement and a desire to watch. But we all know the desire to know what is going on. Who can drive by an accident scene without taking a look at the carnage and in doing so could possible create more carnage? Very few of us. So if our view of the famous is predominately in a negative vein, why would anyone want to be noticed?

Could it be that we are secretly pleased when bad things happen to others, because we were spared? Perhaps, but another way to examine the preponderance of attention to negative things is that it establishes the underpinnings for the thought process that to become famous from negative behavior is much easier than to become famous for proper behavior.

On a scale of one to ten, with one being a total recluse and ten being an unabashed attention seeker, where would you place yourself and your acquaintances? When I was in grade school, although I did not realize it at the time, I sought attention. Doing something negative usually got me into trouble, but it also got me noticed by my classmates. Getting a b+ on an exam went by unnoticed by my classmates. Recently a disturbed young man lost his job serving fast food. He also lost his girlfriend. The school aged young man sought fame as a final act and killed a number of people in a shopping mall before killing himself. For a few days he was famous, although he never knew it. In the distorted mind of the rare school aged child, this thought process is confirmed much too frequently. Suicide amongst young people is such an outcome. It is the act that will get them noticed.

Society has noticed this trend and has attempted to thwart the development of this attention seeking by modifying certain procedures. Youth sports has attempted to remove some of the competitiveness and give a trophy to everyone who plays, thereby removing the disappointment of the child who doesn't get the award for scoring the most goals or being the league's most valuable player. I don't remember anyone in my age group being cured of an emotional problem by being handed a trophy.

Society should be looking at other things. Relationships and families are not what they once were. Children are being raised in absentia. Children learn from television and computers more than they learn from parents. How many parents are dysfunctional and unable to provide adequate guidance for children? Reliance on the educational system is misplaced. Teachers are more likely the products of the same environments that their students emanate from. How can the teachers life experiences translate to a benefit for the student. And, in the event that the teacher is well balanced and would be able to provide training to students, the teacher's hands are tied by ridiculous rules regarding discipline and politically correct speech and behavior.

There is an answer to all of the issues stated above. That answer is discipline. Not discipline for the benefit of the person wielding the control, but discipline for the person learning the lesson. I went into the Navy in 1957. I went to Great Lakes Training Center for what was called "Boot Camp." We were to be formed into "Companies" and "Platoons," but initially we were just a huge group of 17 to 20 years old boys from all over the country. All of us were in "civilian clothes" when we arrived and we spent the better part of the first two days in the clothes. We were given tests, medical exams and did some physical exercises. We marched from place to place. We were all taken to the barbershop where our heads were shaved to about a quarter inch of hair. At that point we were told that we were to be issued our uniforms, but first we had to send our clothes home. Each recruit was given paper and string and a pencil and a label. We stripped off all of our clothes, wrapped them in paper, secured them with string and addressed the label to mail them home.

This was all done in a large gymnasium by nearly five hundred boys. We had been marched into the gymnasium and given a spot to stand which was approximately four feet in each direction from the next fellow. The packages were collected and we were told to sit on the floor all facing in one direction. For the most part we were all strangers to each other. We sat on the floor for more than an hour, but it seemed like a week. There was no conversation. It would have been awkward to try since the others were not only strangers, but were four feet away and you would have had to speak loud enough that many others would have heard you. We were naked and bald. When it was finally over, we were taken in groups to get our uniforms. We came back to the gymnasium and got dressed. There was no conversation concerning the wait. In fact, during all of "Boot Camp" I do not remember discussing that episode with anyone.

It may seem strange to the reader, but it was the first step and a very important step into the discipline required to turn boys into servicemen. No one would question the need for discipline in the military. There is little room for individualism that strays from the goal of the operation. Each person has a duty that when performed is a part of the overall success of the military operation. Some are better at what they do than others, but each must perform to utmost of their ability. The one hour sitting on the gymnasium floor naked and bald, removed us from the people we were and made us military recruits. Gone was the long hair, sideburns, pompadours, engineer boots with cleats, sneakers, motorcycle jackets, T shirts with cigarettes rolled into the sleeve, baseball hats, dungarees worn low on the hip and rolled up at the bottom that symbolized our previous identity. When I think back to that time, I remember feeling so removed from my former self, a teenager who would hang on the corner and smoke cigarettes, that if the sailor in charge of us would have told us to march to Chicago, I and the rest of those fellows would have lined up and began to walk.

Later in life I became a Police Officer and while on duty, was sent to a prison where the prisoners were rioting. The Authorities used the same tactic when control was established, in that they made the prisoners strip. Naked people, it seems, are more responsive to commands and less likely to want to fight.

It is important to note that the discipline instilled in that moment was for the benefit of the Navy. That episode undoubtedly brought us farther along in the process to becoming sailors who would follow orders and perform as requested. But the greatest beneficiary were the boys who became Navy Recruits in that instance and did not require the constant discipline and punishment that would have been necessary to get the corner lounger, football star, lover boy, tough guy, bully, trouble maker, momma's boy, bad kid, to adhere to the rules and policies of the Navy. While the couple of sailors who worked at the "Boot Camp" may have had a laugh or two out of the experience later, there was no benefit to them.

As a society we have seemed to give up on creative discipline. It seems to me that discipline in the home and in the school is administered for the benefit of the one administering the discipline. By the home I mean in the family. I see parents discipline their children in public once in a while and it is easy to see that it is a foreign subject to them. The parent is usually angry and nearing their wit's end when they begin to argue with the child as though reason is going to cure the problem. The parent may beg or plead or threaten. Rarely today do you see any parent physically chastise their child. I have seen parents take their child outside away from prying eyes and can only suspect that there is some type of physical persuasion being administered. Discipline should be an everyday concern for a parent. Discipline should be administered with planning. Organization is discipline. As a supervisor in the Police Department, the officers in my platoon were to be on time and were scheduled for their lunch break at a certain time and had to patrol their sectors exclusively. If they were late, spent more time than they should on lunch break, or worse, were riding or walking somewhere outside of the area they were assigned, they were neglecting their duty. Since spanking was out of the question and I couldn't cause everyone to be fired, creative discipline was necessary. A change of assignment, a no for a day off request, or worse, being a constant presence during their patrol hours was usually enough to make errant behavior reverse itself. I cannot say that officers never made me angry, but I can say that acting out of anger would have been a personal failure for me. As a parent I also tried to not respond out of anger. This doesn't mean that I didn't yell.

When I completed "Boot Camp" and service school, I was assigned to a Destroyer as a machinist mate. I worked in the Engine Room. The noise level in the Engine Room was never measured while I was in the Navy, but I can safely describe it as very noisy. If you wanted to speak to someone while at sea and the machinery was operating, it was necessary to have your face within a foot of the person you were speaking to and then yell at them. Needless to say after three years on the destroyer I had considerable volume. A loud voice is authoritative. There are times when yelling is appropriate and effective. Yelling requires no anger. A good yell gets the persons attention and usually quells an unwanted response.

In the Police Department I was assigned to the Canine Unit. Dog training is discipline of the highest order. Dogs understand some words in the sense that they respond to them. Dogs have a keen sense of smell and an even keener sense of emotion. Dogs recognize immediately a person who likes them and they know who is afraid of them. When I trained my dog (with the help of trainer) I learned to discipline with a word. Initially a physical act accompanied the word, but ultimately only the word was required. We trained on the words "no" and "good boy." To further explain; initially, "no" was spoken simultaneously with tension on the collar, pulling the dog close and then with the hand forcing the rear into a sitting position. After a while "no" made the dog stop what he was doing and come to my side and sit down. When the dog completed the movement to my side and sat down he received a good boy. My dog knew instinctively and from my actions that I loved him. While on patrol, the dog was a better partner than any human. He would unquestionable come to my aid. He had better senses of negative emotions than I did and made his presence known to anyone who harbored such thoughts. My dog always followed my commands. My children were another matter.

Unfortunately, our children are not dogs. We can't control them 24/7 and we are not the only people that they ever have to listen to and be supervised by. However, thinking through a plan of discipline for your child is an important matter. You cannot wait until they anger you to decide that discipline is required. Family dinners have seemed to become a thing of the past. Dinners used to be an important element of discipline and they should be again. Children are taught the proper way to eat. The use of utensils, napkins, manners and courtesy are important parts of the dinner experience. When I was a child we sat down for dinner. First however, my sister and I had to complete our dinner chore. We alternated helping set the table and clearing the table. There was no deviation, it was our job. My sister and I helped to put the food on the table and no one ate until everyone was seated. We were required to say please when requesting that food be passed around the table. We never spoke with food in our mouths. Conversations were started and ended by our parents. In my life I was hit by my father on two occasions and both times I sorely deserved it. If dinner doesn't work for you, you should find a way that enables you to be in charge and to gain the cooperation of your children. The sole thought should be of discipline.

Unfortunately, in this age of television, most children are being raise by Elmo or Big Bird or some other television show. Parents are too engaged in their own selves to be concerned about their children's discipline. Dinners are served in front of the TV so that conversation is not necessary. A drive is not the family affair where children see signs and farms and animals and seek an explanation from their parents. It is instead a time when children stare at the DVD projector hanging from the car ceiling and occupying their minds so that they don't ask, "Are we there yet?"

Have I wandered away from the chapter's theme, greed? No. All of the foregoing points to a lack of structure. Discipline must also contain a "good boy" (or girl). Being acknowledged for a job well done is of utmost importance. A well earned "good boy" is the recognition and acknowledgement that is necessary for a healthy mind and attitude. When everyone wins the trophy it removes the importance of doing something and getting a "good boy." Another way of stating the same thing is to say that success is harder to define over the last few decades of my life. It is especially difficult if one finds it necessary for others to acknowledge success. As a young boy and man, I received acknowledgement from my parents and later from supervisors in the Navy and the Police Department. The latter two were in conjunction with passing promotional examinations and being promoted among other things. While I enjoyed the recognition at the time, over the ensuing years the recognition became less necessary when I realized that a personal "good boy" was truly much more important. Recognizing my own worth is far more rewarding than the praise of someone else, who may have their own agenda for heaping compliments at me. But I don't feel that many people are satisfied with complimenting themselves.

Therein is the core of the problem that brings about the overwhelming desire for wealth and fame. So much of the daily toil of life is performed for us that building a framework of small successes that would lead to a positive attitude toward ourselves is difficult. Laser guided power saws eliminate the expertise of being able to saw a straight line. A laser level makes hanging shelves a breeze. The computer does a mathematical problem in the blink of an eye. The microwave cooks dinner, and on and on. Showing our personal worth to the world (even the small world that represents our lives) is almost impossible. People who have achieved (?) fame in many cases are not people that we would look up to. Many of the famous people that are reported upon day after day, live lives of disaster. Finding a positive aspect to their lives is difficult if not impossible. It can in a distorted way seem that the measure of success is simply to be rich and famous without the need to succeed. It is not just the deranged youngster who takes a gun to school or the shopping mall, it is many of the youngsters who yearn to be acknowledged with a good boy or girl who give up hope of being able to attain such praise.

Speed

I alluded to speed in the first chapter and won't labor the point here. But it must be pointed out that we have as a society accomplished more in the last hundred years than was accomplished in the previous five thousand. All of this accomplishment in such a short time has created some unfortunate side effects. Let me explain.

Lindbergh made the first non-stop flight across the Atlantic Ocean in the early part of the 1900s. Life at that time was, compared to today, the dark ages. We carry cell phones that can connect us to people in almost any corner of the world. Doctors can look at pictures of our bones without cutting us open. None of which was possible in 1908. Nothing, however, comes without a price tag. Now that we can communicate at any time day or night with others, we have made it necessary to do so. Now that we can drive hundreds of miles in a day we have made it necessary. Now that we can e-mail someone across the globe in seconds it is necessary. All of the foregoing have created a state of mind that requires instantaneous responses. We have no patience. In the 1800s fields were plowed with a horse. Seeds were planted and the wait was on. There was plenty to do around the farm but crops required patience. The pace of life was slower. A trip to visit relatives was a vast undertaking. The people of the 1800s had to be patient. Their lives were taken a step at a time. When you had children in those times, depending on the type of life you lived, the children were trained to help around the house and then trained to help in the earning of a living. The children knew that they had to learn the trade of their parents as their very lives depended upon it. Children were instilled with discipline. Discipline was required to manage the household and the continuation of the life cycle.

In my daily commute I see hundreds of other drivers. Many have put to use the time spent in the automobile. Driving is not enough. Make-up must be applied. Books and newspapers must be read. And phone conversations must be held. To say that these distractions have caused pain, injury and in the worst case, death is stating the obvious. However, there is more to the story. All of our waking hours must be filled with distractions. We no longer value idle time. When we are idle we become bored and seek a distraction. The most likely distraction is the television.

When I was a child we watched television, but not until I was about ten years old. I was born in 1939 and television came to our house about 1949. The first decade or more of television was limited to just a couple of channels with few real selections The shows were closely monitored for content. I recently read that the first couple shown in the same bed were Fred and Wilma Flintstone. In the other family shows the parents either had twin beds or separate rooms and always wore pajamas. Otherwise the filming stopped at the bedroom door. Leave it to Beaver, Make Room for Daddy, Father Knows Best were some of the original shows. They had a message that was meant to be instructive as well as entertaining. Bad language was not acceptable, even in motion pictures. The movie entitled "On the Waterfront" starring Marlon Brando was released in the fifties and created a furor because Marlon Brandon told Carl Malden (playing a priest) to go to Hell. Needless to say clothing of the actors in the movies was also controlled.

Today almost anything goes. Bad language, skimpy clothing, sexual plots are all the norm. The message, if any, is lost in the titillating or violent behavior of the cast. We watch regardless. We are unable to entertain ourselves by reading or heaven forbid having a discussion that would enhance the family relationship. Our children are taught at birth to seek the distraction of television. They are plopped in front of the television while they eat, do homework, or idle away time. The television keeps them from fidgeting as babies with constant talk and action and to a large extent replaces family instruction, discussion and relationships as the children age. Children probably learn more from Sesame Street than their parents.

Children are plopped in front of the television because we don't have the time to spend with them. If you are middle aged or older, think back to the time you spent with your parents. Breakfast, dinner, homework, weekday evenings, were probably spent to a large degree with parents interested in what you were doing. Parents today expect the television, the teacher, or some other entity to raise the children, because, despite all of the time saving devices around the home and in our daily lives, we have no time. There is more information in the standard home computer than can be found in any library. (This is stated as a belief and not a fact) With basic knowledge of the computer we can review in seconds materials that we would have to have spent hours researching in the library. But for the most part, we are not researching educational or work related information, we are exploring the web. We can chat with total strangers concerning their problems or beliefs in anonymity but we cannot speak to our children or other family members with the same openness. How come? My answer to that question is that it is easier to be anonymous. If someone is looking you in the eye, telling lies or exaggerating is much more difficult. If an internet conversation becomes tense or uncomfortable you can simply move to another screen location.

Many years ago people lived in homes with their extended family. Grandparents, parents and children often lived in the same residence. I lived during that period and my memory tells me that people were much more civil. The controlling mentality was what might be referred to as the "small town" mentality. It is always said that when you live in a small town everyone knows everyone else's business. I grew up in Philadelphia, which at the time of my childhood had a population of over two million people. Today it has shrunk to one million four hundred thousand. Despite the large size of the city, we lived in neighborhoods that could have been small towns. We knew our neighbors and communicated with them on a daily basis. We called neighbors aunt and uncle despite the fact that they were not related. In some instances they knew more about our family than our real relatives because of the proximity and the daily communication.

Our community in Philadelphia was our small town. When everyone in town knows everyone's business, it is harder to be uncivil. Breaking the law or acting in an unacceptable fashion spread through town like wildfire and the opinions formed lasted for some time. The violator would have to make amends if they want to live in harmony with the community. Today we don't have the enforcement of morals and mores from outside of our own heads. We don't share a relationship with neighbors, relatives or others to the extent that we would care if they found our conduct unacceptable. A microcosm of our society can be readily found on our highways. There is a total lack of civility when driving a car. We are in a rush to get there, no matter where there is. Someone driving slow deserves the middle digit, the horn, a snarling face, or some screamed obscenity. Finding a way to sneak ahead of someone in line is a coup not rudeness. Taking advantage of every situation for some perceived benefit is a way of life. It has to be easy and it has to be fast.

When we talk to young people today it is easy to discern that they feel that success must be obtained in an instant, regardless of the perceived meaning of success. Within weeks or months of starting a new position or "job," it becomes obvious to the young person that they are the only person employed with any sense. All of the people who supervise them are idiots and should be moved aside so that the young person can replace them and show them how the business, organization, or whatever the employment function is, should be run. There is an immediate dissatisfaction with pay, responsibility, etc. The company is wasting my talent. No one there is smart enough to recognize superior talent. The bad part of this is that in today's electronic world it is unfortunately true in some limited circumstances. The seventeen year old who grew up staring at a computer is far more adept at getting the most out of the device than someone who is just getting used to the idea that pay phones are gone and cell phones are necessary and useful. However, the fact that in rare cases someone at a very young age can handle a complex task in the adult world does not make it right. Discipline is lost to the speedy progression of a young worker.

When I was growing up adults were always, or almost always right. My parents, as well as the parents of all of my friends, made it clear that we were to respect our elders. There was a woman who lived by herself about a block from my home. She resided in a corner property that occupied the inside corner of an ell shaped intersection. The street that passed in front of her home continued past the intersecting street for about 60 feet and dead ended at a railroad track. The railroad was elevated about 25 to 30 feet above the street level on a man made hill covered with stones which were half the size of a baseball. Baseball is what we played on the dead end street. Occasionally someone would hit a ball that would land in her side yard. Neither I nor any of my friends were brave enough to attempt to retrieve the ball if we could not reach it without setting foot on her property. We called her the "Grouch." If anyone went into her yard she would seem to know instinctively and would immediately appear in the doorway and yell at who possessed the temerity to violate her rules. In most instances we would run away. We knew that in any confrontation with an adult we would lose. The adult would most assuredly tell our parents and we would be punished. No explanation would alter the course of events.

Times have changed. Children go home and tell their parents that the teacher doesn't like them and the parents believe the children. Parents yell at sports coaches coaching their children for any perceived infraction. Not playing enough or playing too much can be the perceived infraction. The tone of voice that the coach uses to correct the child when an error is committed can bring on the wrath of the parent, occasionally with tragic consequences. Why is this happening today. Simply because of speed or, said in a different way because it will require the parent to spend time explaining the actions of the coach. We are so into time usage that we do not have the patience to spend time disciplining our children. We want teachers to do it. Raising our children and teaching them right from wrong is the schools responsibility. If not the school then it is the job of television. But it cannot be ours. We have to use our time doing something of benefit to ourselves, such as communicating with strangers on the internet.

Discipline requires time. Discipline requires attention. Discipline requires planning. To effectively bring discipline into the life of our children benefits us as well as them. When I say it benefits us, I am not talking about the reduction of stress when a child learns to control their own lives. I am talking about the strengthening of our own individual discipline. The impatience that we have because of the slow procedure at work to recognize our superior talent and pay us what we are worth, can sometimes fall into prospective. When we explain the benefits of performance, temper modification, patience and the ability to put one's self in the posture of the other person, it could lead us to some understanding of our own situation that would yield benefit.

Our lives not only require planning, but also require review. Many years ago while in undergraduate school, I talked my counselor into allowing me to take a series of psychology courses. I was in the School of Business, with a sub-major in Law Enforcement. The courses were to replace electives, which would normally be my choice, however, these courses were in a graduate program. The titles of the courses were, Group Dynamics" and "The Analysis of Group Participation". The first led to the second, and provided the groundwork for appreciating the second, but I feel that I personally gained more from the second course than any other course that I took the entire time I was in college. The first night of the course which was three hours, no one took charge of the course. The night school class consisted of a wide age range, but included no one of undergraduate age. We were all at least in our late twenties and some were nearing fifty. It was easy for the professor to be present and not be recognized.

As college students, we were concerned about getting credits. We were concerned about being registered for a course that did not seem to be happening. We wondered aloud whether we would have time to register for another course in the same time slot. We discussed what the rule was for being credited for attendance when the professor did not show up. Some said we had to wait at least a half an hour. Someone else produced a tablet that we all began to sign to show that we had in fact been in the classroom. We fidgeted and fumed but no one left for the first forty-five minutes. Then a young woman walked in and said she was a teaching assistant and that the class was in fact going to be held in that time slot and we should all appear the following week.

The next week the chairs were assembled in a circle and again no one appeared to be in charge. We began to talk. At first we talked to anyone that we knew in the class. Some people, however, knew no one from any previous classes and they joined into conversation already in progress. Most of the conversations were not related to psychology except for wondering what was going to be required to obtain a good grade for this course. After more than an hour of random conversation, the professor identified himself and told us the course requirements. The first requirement was attendance. Failure to attend regularly would result in a failure. A term paper would bring about a medium grade, and if the paper was any good it would yield a superlative grade. There was no preparation necessary to attend class, and reading materials would be determined at a later date. The professor then asked some of the students about their conversations. He then sought comments from others concerning the explanations.

Week after week without seeming to have any structure this class went forward. Sometimes the professor would be late and we would begin to talk amongst ourselves. When he would arrive he would catch someone in the middle of a statement and would encourage them to finish their thought. With little encouragement we would continue the conversation feeling that the longer we talked the less he would talk, and therefore, it was less likely he would get to anything substantive. Sometime after about four weeks, the class conversation began to develop into more than conversation. Groups were being formed that supported an opinion voiced by a class member. Other groups opposed the position. Individuals began to disagree. Opinions began to be challenged. Pontification was running rampant. It was at this point that the word introspection was introduced to the class. Introspect is defined as a look inside, to examine one's own mind reflectively. This brought about a great number of questions which started out as, "Why did you say that?" and ended with "Why did you ask why I said that?" Needless to say the tone of the conversation became more intense and in some cases heated. No one missed a class, because to do so would be yielding your position on whatever the issue was when the class ended. The three hours went by in a flash and we were usually interrupted by the professor to say that class was over and we would pick up where we left off next week.

I for one took introspection to heart. I would review what I said and try to determine why I said it. My answer was not always clear cut. There could be multiple motivations for saying something or commenting about a statement of someone else. For example, when a teacher is teaching a class about a subject that the teacher knows well, is the teacher imparting wisdom or trying to impress the students with their knowledge of the subject. When a student who has carefully studied the upcoming lesson keeps raising his/her hand to inform the teacher and the rest of the class that he/she has knowledge of the subject, is it being helpful or just a form of bragging.

Introspection of one's self leads to better understanding, not only of yourself, but of others. Understanding your motivation is to instill discipline in yourself. Most people do not want to harm others. Most people are not trying to be rude and insulting. It is more likely that they have not taken the time to determine why another driver is going so slow in the passing lane. When you try to put yourself in the position of the person in front of you going slow, you might remember the last time you were on a trip on a strange highway and were overcome by uncertainty about where you should turn. I have been in both situations. I can't say that I am always considerate of the other guy, but I do try. Introspection, however, requires time and we don't seem to have any.

GOVERNMENT

A great deal of what we think and do is related to the government. When the expansion to the West occurred, Americans had very little to do with the government. There were government programs that granted people enough ground for a homestead, but there was no town planning board to tell you where on your property you could build your home. Nor did anyone tell you that your home had to be a certain number of square feet, and could not be bigger than a certain number of square feet.

Over the years since then we have developed and enlarged the four types of government that oversee our actions. They are National, State, County and Local government bodies. Each of which has many branches and many functions. Each has the power to enact laws to control our behavior and oversee our property rights. Each has the power to police us to insure that we follow the laws that they enact. Each has the power to form a judicial body to rule on the system of enforcing the laws that are enacted. Each of these bodies have enacted laws that create other types of governance (bureaucracies) that are very often free of government control and often times are at odds with the governing body that created them. There are many examples of this strange creation, for example, the Environmental Protection Agencies. Another example would be the Public Defenders Association. The strange part of this is that the agencies sometimes sue the government that empowers them, citing the fact that the government is in violation of the law. These cases can find their way to the highest court in land, after exhausting all of the other courts along the way. The process of the legal procedure can take many years and involve many lawyers and legal staffs in preparation for the trial. Interestingly enough, in many of those cases all of the participants are paid from taxpayer dollars. Some might argue that these cases are in our best interest. In some cases those arguments might have merit. However, it still seems strange that the government sues itself to force it to do the right thing.

Sometimes the State government and the Federal government sue each other. For example, the State is responsible for education. The Federal government has programs that give money to the States for education. The Federal government then enacts laws concerning education in the States. The Federal government creates a bureaucracy to enforce the laws and police the States. The States sue for the educational funds and the Federal government sues to enforce the requirements that the Federal Government has created. All of the lawyers and all of the judges are government employees. All of both of the staffs supporting the lawyers on both sides and the staffs of the court are government employees. For the most part, all of the witnesses who testify are either employees of the government or paid with taxpayer's dollars. I wonder if Washington, Jefferson, Adams and all of the others who met in Philadelphia to form this government had this in mind.

Benjamin Franklin published a magazine called "Poor Richard's Almanack," which was full of common sense material and sayings. It would seem that it should be read before the start of each governmental session of any legislative body. We could surely use some common sense. Webster defines common sense as "sound and prudent but often unsophisticated judgment." Before jumping to the conclusion that Webster was saying something negative about common sense you have to read the definition of sophistication from the same book. Webster lists four examples, #1 the use of sophistry: sophistic reasoning; #2 the process of making impure or weak; #3 the process or result of becoming cultured, knowledgeable, or disillusioned; #4 the process or result of becoming more complex, developed or subtle.

In today's world we seem to feel that everything is complex and beyond our ability to understand. Some of that thought process comes from medicine, science and engineering. Unless you are a part of those fields, you would be in the dark if you overheard a conversation between scientists, doctors or engineers. I would like to convince you that the world is no more complex than it was a hundred years ago, or at least not in the sense of its application to government. I am a lawyer. Most of the people who are running our government are lawyers or have some association with the law. I would venture to say that many of those who possess a law degree, after twelve years of schooling as a child and at least seven more years as an adult, cannot change the oil in their automobile or fix a flat tire. Nor can they install a new kitchen or bathroom faucet. They probably couldn't successfully grow a tomato plant or a cantaloupe. Human beings long ago realized that they couldn't perform every function in life. There were builders and there were hunters. There were fishermen and there were boat builders. Some people are multi-talented and others are not. Those who are not are still able to understand all of things that are necessary to live in today's world. We don't have to understand why a computer functions to use it. What you are reading here is being written by me typing the words into a computer. I would classify myself as someone who is mechanically inclined. I understand how things work and how they can be fixed. That does not, however, include the computer and other electronic devices. I have removed the back or side of electronic devices and I can see where the electricity goes in, but I cannot see anything moving inside. I don't know why anything happens inside the computer because I cannot follow the path of information or energy with just my sight. I'd like to think that if I felt it was important to me I could learn, but I obviously don't feel it is that important.

Life itself can be understood in simplistic terms. We need to eat, drink and breathe to live. We have extended our lifespan over those who preceded us due to the technologies which control nature's elements effect on us, and technologies which help us to prevent disease and live healthier lives. Interaction between governments should also be viewed in simplistic terms. Our government is doing the same things which governments have been saying and doing since the first person took charge over others.

Going to war requires no special ability. War is taking conflict to the extreme. Countries have gone to war over property and over trade.

Countries have gone to war over power or the threat of power. All of the elements leading up to war can be examined in the abstract and compared to a segment of our lives. When we were children there was invariably someone who was a bully. The bully, for whatever reason he might have had, wanted to exercise power over others. Sometimes, the bully would underestimate the will of someone he was bullying and would have his clock cleaned. Other times the person or persons being bullied would seek the help of someone else to force the bully to leave them alone. That person providing aid may have been a teacher, a parent or just another child. There were bullies who did not respond to people who tried to intervene because they had more going on in their heads than simply trying to show someone they could exert power.

There are people in Africa, the Middle East and in the countries that used to make up the U.S.S.R. who are terrible bullies. These people are exerting power over those with less power in terrible and tragic ways. Their alleged motivation could be anything, such as religion, ethnicity, property or trade to name a few, but they are at heart bullies. These people are only different from the street thug who intimidates and robs old people in our own country by the magnitude of their crimes. These people are abusing power. A street thug in the U.S. might be an addict of some sort, or could be a sociopath, but that would make little difference to the person who is the victim.

We have gone to war with a bully who wanted to control the world. Hitler was a bully personified. He amassed power over Germany and then extended that power to rule his neighbors with an eye on ruling the world. Since the Second World War, we have experienced conflict on a number of occasions without having the conflict come to the same conclusion that the Second World War did. The only conflict that seemed to accomplish what it set out to do was the First Gulf War. Iraq invaded Kuwait and we came to the aid (along with other countries) of Kuwait. We stopped and reversed the invasion. The President was criticized for not unseating Saddam Hussien and lost the right to have a second term in office. None of the remaining conflicts (wars) have been successful. Most of us in this country have no idea why we fought in Korea, Vietnam, Kosovo or other places.

On the surface the Korean conflict was to stop the invasion of South Korea by the North Koreans. The North Koreans were supported by the Chinese. We were not the only country fighting in this conflict. In the end, the North Koreans went north of the 38th parallel and we still have people there making sure they don't try to come back over. We have been watching that line since 1955. Without laboring this point, a study of our recent history and a study of world history back to the beginning of recorded history would force us to conclude that there have always been bullies and apparently there will always be bullies. The question that our government seems unable to answer is how to effectively deal with a bully. Perhaps the decision should be made after talking with an elementary school teacher or a parent. Maybe we are in our own way a bully.

War is not the only thing that our government seems inept at handling. They are equally or more inept at handling the business affairs of government. The first example I want to give is a microcosm of the overall problem. I was in the U.S. Navy from 1957 to 1960. During that time I served on a destroyer that operated out of Norfolk, Virginia and Charleston, South Carolina. My job on the ship was that of a machinist mate. I worked in one of the two engine rooms on the ship. The engine room housed a huge turbine driven by steam. The turbine was the power that turned the starboard propeller. There were also a number of other steam turbines that operated supporting machinery. During my time in the Navy, my mother was employed by Sears. Sears sells tools under the brand name of Craftsman. We had many Craftsman tools at home as a result of her employment, since we were able to obtain them at a discount in the employer's store. I especially liked Craftsman tools because they were guaranteed for life. If you broke a Craftsman tool you could return it for a new one.

The engine room in which I worked was supervised by a machinist mate who had the rank of first-class petty officer. The engine room had a budget. I am sure that the ship's budget was divided up amongst the varying units on the ship, but I had personal knowledge of only the engine room in which I worked. The first thing I learned in the Navy about government funds was, that if you were budgeted a certain amount of money you spent it all. The theory behind that logic was that should you not spend it, your budget would be reduced the following year. In the latter period of my stay on the ship, I was a third class petty officer and the engine room supervisor handed me the catalog and told me to spend or order enough from the catalog to bring the engine room total up to our budget limit. When I looked at the prices of the tools I was astounded. The tools which were not anywhere near the quality of Craftsman tools were three times the price of Craftsman tools. Furthermore, there was no guarantee.

The second example is the management of money by the Federal government. Assume that you worked for a private, non-government employer that took a percentage of your pay to start a retirement fund. Each week when you got your check that percentage would be removed. The employer told you that he was putting an equal amount, matching your funds, into the retirement account. After working at the company for many years you came to learn that the pension fund money did not exist. In the private sector, your employer would be arrested.

However, in the government sector nothing happens. We have been paying into the Social Security Fund for years and none of the money, not the contribution taken from your pay, nor the matching contribution made by your employer, goes into the fund. It could be used to pay current recipients of Social Security or it goes into the general fund and is spent along with all of the other tax dollars. The fund was only a fund until the middle sixties when it was depleted by our own government.

In Philadelphia there is a pension fund. Employees contribute six percent of their pay and the City must also contribute by some convoluted formula that is vague for reasons known only to the City. However, despite that fact, the pension fund is stable and secure and pays benefits far in excess of the schedule of payments found through Social Security.

If the Social Security Fund would have been preserved, there not only would be no threat to Americans that it won't be there, but given the fact the Philadelphia is able to pay a benefit in excess of what Social Security pays after collecting far less, it would stand to reason that Social Security recipients maybe could afford to stop eating pet food.

I don't use Philadelphia as an example of exemplary government. There was a time when the City government wanted to dip into the fund. The fund is managed by employees and outside contractors, and they sued to prevent the incursion and won. Furthermore, Philadelphia, like many other governments in this country, is outspending its ability to collect taxes. Philadelphia was, in the fifties and sixties, a city with a population of over two million. The population has shrunk to less than one million five hundred thousand. During those same fifty plus years the size of the government and the government payroll has grown exponentially. And that's in both real dollars and inflationary dollars.

I had the same experience in Philadelphia Police Department that I had while in the Navy. At the end of a budget year, you had to order supplies in order to use your entire budget. The same prevailing logic existed. Should you fail to spend it all you will have less to spend next year.

There are many examples at the federal and state level of taxes that are imposed for a specific purpose, but eventually find their way into the general fund. Later, when the money is needed for the purpose it was intended, the government floats a bond or goes further into debt. Wouldn't it be great if we could each run our lives the way the governments run the business of government? We could buy a huge house with a swimming pool and a tennis court. Buy a yacht and an expensive car and finance the whole thing. It wouldn't matter if we couldn't afford to pay the finance charge. We could just go to our boss and tell him/her to raise our pay sufficiently to cover the payment. Or once a month when the payment becomes due, we could simply borrow the money to make the payment. Who cares what will happen in the future, it will be someone else's problem.

Why don't we exercise more care in selecting the people who run the government? Mainly it's because we don't have too much to do with the selection process. During my tenure as a Philadelphia Police Officer, I was assigned to investigate applicants for the job of Police Officer. The first part of the application for the job was to take a civil service examination. After a candidate passed that portion, the investigative unit examined the candidate's background. The first step of the process was for the candidate to fill out a questionnaire. The candidate had to account for all of the time that had elapsed from the time he/she finished high school. The candidate also provided the name of the school attended (high school, college, trade school, etc.) and signed a permission slip to allow the investigator to see the records of schooling. The investigator then talked to teachers and employers and examined records from each school or employment. The investigator also talked to neighbors and to the references listed on the candidate's application form. Finally, prior to an offer of employment as a Police Officer, the candidate was required to take a polygraph examination where one of the questions was, "Did you answer the candidate questionnaire truthfully?" Needless to say, we had a pretty good idea of the person before they were hired. (Incidentally, at the time of this writing the polygraph is no longer used).

If you talked to a citizen of Philadelphia about the hiring process for a Philadelphia Police Officer, they would probably agree that the process was a good one. That is not to say that everyone who got the job was a good officer. Some people are not suited to be Police Officers. It is not the right job for a bully, despite the fact that bullies sometimes aspire to be Police Officers because of the power involved in the job.

What about senators, congressmen, mayors, council people, and even presidents? If Philadelphia was that concerned about someone they were hiring to patrol the streets and protect the public, should we not be as concerned about someone who is enacting laws and spending trillions of our tax dollars. (I have been retired for some time and can not speak to the current process).

While I am writing this there is a presidential election underway. The field of candidates has been thinned and there are two republicans, two democrats and an independent. One candidate was in the armed services, but I can not say whether any of the others were. Four of the five candidates are currently in the service of the government (elected by their constituents), but I don't know if any ever had a job for anyone other than the government. I know that hundreds of millions of dollars have been spent already on this campaign and hundreds of millions more will be spent before it's over. In the end one will win and take office and perhaps involve us in some type of conflict and will most assuredly take part is spending trillions of our tax dollars. And yet we don't even ask them to take a polygraph examination.

Why does it have to be this way? We are looking for someone to deal with the bullies of the rest of the world. We are looking for someone to manage the government without throwing our tax money down a rat hole. We need a person who can act as the CEO of this enterprise. There is not a CEO in the world who handles the type of money that the president handles in his annual budget. Nor does any CEO have the number of employees that the president has amongst the many people paid by the U.S. government. And yet, the president is paid four hundred thousand dollars a year. Makes you stop and think. Many of the people taking the oath of office to be president are already rich and don't need the money. On the other hand no one leaves the office poor. Speaking engagements provide huge paydays for someone who has been president. I often thought that it was strange that a person would spend hundreds of millions of dollars to get a job that for the four years in office paid only one million six hundred thousand. But then I realized that they were spending, for the most part, other people's money.

That brings up another point that defies common sense. Why would anyone contribute to the campaign of someone who was going to be their employee? In its simplest terms the candidates are looking for a job. While it is hard to truly get the feeling that we, the voters, and even those amongst us who don't vote, are the employers, by our votes we are hiring these folks to be our president. If you contribute five hundred or a thousand, you must expect that you will be in a preferential place in the candidate's heart when they take office. The defiance of common sense is how could that happen when it requires more than hundreds of millions of dollars. Therefore, if your contribution was one thousand you would have given between 1/100,000th and perhaps 1/600,000th of what was spent. But then maybe you really are just seeking good government.

All this talk of money has made me think of something else, foreign aid. While I am a proponent of charity, I am hard pressed to figure who is receiving the charity of foreign aid. Recently it was reported that the United States gave ten Billion dollars to Pakistan. More correctly, the report said that we gave it to the president of Pakistan. I am aware that in a country such as ours when a basketball player can earn a hundred million dollars for a multi-year contract and presidential candidates can spend more than five or six hundred million to get elected (and even lose), ten billion can be overlooked. From another vantage point, however, it seems huge. Social Security is broke, we cannot properly equip our troops in the field and we are being taxed at an enormous rate. (Later on I will talk about the amount of tax that we pay) Now clearly, we would not object to giving ten billion dollars to Pakistan if we are shown that it benefits the Pakistanis and somehow from that benefit, we as a country receive a benefit. But I don't recall being shown anything. Almost anything would probably make giving away ten billion more palatable such as when we make a contribution to a charity at home and we are shown the pictures of the children or people that are helped by our generosity. We can deservedly get a good feeling. But Pakistan has not shown us anything, at least not me.

So, I can tell you without reservation that I get no such feeling relative to any of our foreign aid. No one living outside of the United States and even some living in the United States seem to like us anymore. Maybe they never did. We have been giving aid to foreign countries for years and if we are trying to buy friends it doesn't seem to be working. Furthermore, I have never be told by anyone in government (and I don't mean personally), who gets the money and what is it being spent on. Now I know that we have given away some of our military hardware to people outside of the United States. We gave a bunch to aid the war in Afghanistan when they were fighting the Russians, but then they used the hardware against us later. I also know that we send food and water and other forms of aid, troops, etc. when there is a natural disaster. But for the most part we aren't told how much money is going to foreign aid and what it is being spent on. Recently the government admitted that our own welfare system was misguided in that it produced a side effect of fatherless homes because the payments were restricted to one parent families. It took fifty years to conclude that the program was misguided. Maybe we shouldn't wait fifty years to look as carefully at the money we are spending outside of the United States. Just a thought.

Back at the start of all this government, the Forefathers decided that we needed to separate the three branches of government. Each should have a certain amount of independence. The President can veto a bill, but the Congress can override the veto. The Court can rule that a piece of legislation is unconstitutional. They also wanted all of us to be properly represented. The Senate was made up of the elite (so-to-speak) and the House was made up of the more everyday folks. I am sure that at the beginning it was tough to leave the farm and come to Philadelphia to deal with the business of government. The senators and representatives had to come by horse or horse and wagon. No private jets with stewardesses bringing cocktails and such. When I was taught American History 101 those many years ago, I was taught that the Congress met seasonally. This was done so that the business of the farm could be taken care of as well as the business of government. Today I wouldn't venture a guess as to how many actual hours senators and congressmen spend on the business of government. They all have staffs that do research and communicate with other staffs concerning upcoming legislation. It would be interesting to know how much we pay for the staffs of each of our legislators. I am sure it would put us all into sticker shock.

The senators and congressmen spend a great deal of time raising money. They must have a constant supply of campaign funds heading into their vaults, since they will spend lots of money when the time comes to be re-elected. I am sure that in the minds of the senators and the congressmen, they consider that a part of the job. Just as they consider legislation that is meant for the home district and legislation that directly benefits a campaign contributor as the business they were elected to perform. I think, though, that if we compared what senators and congressmen were doing in the latter part of the seventeen hundreds and what senators and congressmen are doing now it would be hard to relate one to the other.

How did we get so far afield? Think back to the first two chapters, greed and speed. The Iowans and the New Englanders are probably the only folks who have hands- on feelings about their representatives. Unless you work in the campaign or contribute largely to the campaign, you don't get to see the people who are your representatives up close and personal. They all have handlers. Image Makers. People who advise them what to say and what not to say. People who get their good stories in the press and try to keep the bad ones out. An elected representative would not say that the Union representing a workforce in their home district or state was acting improperly. Unions who pressed for higher wages and benefits for their members and dramatically changed the dynamic in the local workforce would not be criticized by a person who needed the endorsement of the Union and, especially, the campaign contribution of the Union. We are left to read the canned statements of the representatives that may or may not represent their true feelings. We are left to filter through the varying opinions of talk radio, opinion pieces in the newspaper and the slanted reporting on television. We have turned the important business of government into a second Hollywood. Election to national office brings about a star type of adulation from fans. Preparation for a campaign involves speech class, make up and hair dos. Shaking the hand of a senator is like shaking the hand of movie star. In the same vein, thinking that our elected representative is the person that appears behind the podium and is saying what he/she actually thinks, is like thinking that Sylvester Stallone is really Rambo.

How do we change things? The following is my idea. Is it possible that it could really happen? Not very likely. However, it is still my idea and like the ones that follow in other chapters I am proposing the idea as much to make us think outside box, as I am recommending it.

We should eliminate campaign funds totally. It should be illegal to hand our elected representatives or anyone in their cadre money. A person who wants to run for office should be required to obtain signatures from at least a certain number of the voters of the state, county or locality in which they intend to run. Newspapers, radio and television would run, on an equal time basis, the resumes of a candidate and position papers of the candidate. The taxpayers would foot the bill. Anyone who thinks that we are not paying for the campaigns of all these folks is either living in cave, or just has not thought it through properly. When I previously said that maybe a campaign contributor just wants good government, I was kidding. Now surely that doesn't mean that the people who donate fives, tens and hundreds are realistically seeking benefit from the representative, but those big contributors are getting preferential treatment from the government that they convert into cash earnings. Paying three times the value for a tool instead of buying a tool guaranteed for life is one method of repaying a generous contributor. Since there is only the president and vice president who run nationally, a similar system could be devised to obtain an adequate pool of candidates for the offices. In recent years, Governors, Senators, Generals and even a rare Congressperson or Business executive seem to make up the candidate pool. Each potential candidate could obtain a sufficient number of signatures from the state he/she represents or resides in along with the states that are contiguous to that state. Those residents would know the person best. After accomplishing that, the candidate would be considered a candidate and would obtain the privilege of using the media at taxpayers' expense.

We should have paid investigators who would have the job of verifying the statements of a resume. The investigator would have the power to request a polygraph if the statements cannot be verified through investigation. If someone who wants to be a police officer and wield the arrest powers can be forced to take a polygraph, the person who has control over the multi-trillion dollars of our budget and can send our troops to war can take a polygraph. I recently heard a caller to talk radio describe a presidential candidate as someone who would not be able to obtain a security clearance if he/she was in the military. Certainly, someone striving for the office of President should undergo such a screening.

You might think that we would lose the quality candidate if such stringent rules were put in place. I strongly doubt it. Back in the sixties a man named Shapp wanted to become, and did in fact become, the Governor of Pennsylvania. It was reported that he spent millions of his own dollars to get elected. Governor Corzine spent millions of his own money to become senator and governor for the State of New Jersey. More recently Governor Romney spent millions of his own money to mount an unsuccessful campaign for the nomination. Millions of dollars versus a polygraph, unless someone is lying it's a no-brainer.

All of the trappings would remain the same. Being powerful is a strong aphrodisiac. Being famous and in control would certainly be a lure to the job. Having the big house and a bunch of people waiting on you and protecting you would have to seem rather nice. Flying all over the world and having the band play when you walk into a room would bring a flush to your cheek. The only thing you would be able to do and more importantly would have to do, is legislate favorable things for your contributors, just like now, except you would legislate favorable things for the entire country because we would all be the contributors.

Some of you might think that this would raise our taxes. We would be responsible to pay the money that these folks currently spend on elections. Well you are wrong. First, we wouldn't spend the same amount of money. These candidates have, as examples shown earlier, spent huge sums of money to run for office. If viewed properly, as an application for employment, it would require much less. The current party systems would be a jumping off point for someone trying to run for office. The candidate would have to get signatures of a reasonable number of qualified voters to qualify to run. Once qualified the candidate would submit a resume to the all of the newspapers who serve the area in which the electorate reside. The resume could run weekly through the ten weeks prior to the primary election. In addition to the candidate's resume, each week the candidate would be given space to attach a position paper relative to what he/she would hope to accomplish or disassemble if elected. The television and radio stations serving the area of the electorate would broadcast debates among the candidates at least twice prior to the election. Tax dollars would pay the cost of the newspaper print and space and television and radio time.

It could actually enhance the electorate's feeling of participation. I for one have nothing to say about who is going to run for office and represent me at the local, state or federal level. While I am an avid reader of political matters, I have concluded that whenever I voice an interest it is immediately followed by solicitations for money. I have seen over the many years that I have been alive collectively months and months of political commercials. They stink. They are usually grossly unfair to the person being characterized as a crook, a mad person or worse. Some of the worst that I remember were in the presidential election between Lyndon Johnson and Barry Goldwater. Barry Goldwater's position on the Vietnam conflict was that if we were there to fight then fight with all of our might, if not, get out. The issue that developed and was used against Barry Goldwater was the use of low grade nuclear weapons by the military in the day to day conflicts. Barry Goldwater said yes the military should use everything at their disposal. Lyndon Johnson said no and typified the use of nuclear weapons as a choice that only a politician should make. The ad used to exemplify the issue was a cute little girl of six or seven holding a daisy, while a huge nuclear explosion occurred in the background. It was effective. Lyndon Johnson won. However, shortly after President Johnson took office an incident occurred wherein it was claimed that a U.S. Naval Ship (a destroyer, frigate or some other smaller warship) was fired upon. We have always responded ferociously when our ships are attacked or alleged to be attacked. (We went to war over the explosion of the Maine. It is still disputed as to whether it was an accident or an attack) In any case the U.S. went to war against Vietnam (the north) and lost many good men. It was a war of limitations, just like the other wars that we either lost or tied. And we came home without a victory.

In any case, the candidates' ads would be of the nature that he/she would be providing information about himself/herself as to why we would be wise to pick him/her. The election police would present information concerning the veracity of the claims only if they were misstatements. For example, if a candidate espoused health care for all or prescription care for all, the cost of the program would have to accompany the claim. The election investigators would provide separate comment concerning the financial claims. I for one would not miss being inundated with stupid claims of politicians regarding the opposing candidate. After watching most commercials, a reasonable person would have to conclude, either neither was telling the truth or they should both be in jail.

Perhaps if our elected officials were elected by the foregoing standards they would feel a stronger obligation to us as a whole and less to some powerful and rich person. Maybe they would not create so many bureaucracies for their relatives and friends and the unemployable children and relatives of their former contributors. I wrote a paper for a class when I was in a master's program in public administration. I remember the gist of quote but not who to credit for it, but it went like this, "Bureaucracies, once formed, tend to work toward their own survival." (I think it's paraphrased too.) Maybe if we knew what the bureaucracies were supposed to be accomplishing, we would agree with the expenditure. But maybe if we knew what they were actually accomplishing we would have a kitten.

The last thing that I want to talk about in this chapter is taxes. During this presidential primary there is talk of a fair tax, a federal sales tax and disposing of the I.R.S. The I.R.S. is blamed for enforcing the tax code. They are also blamed for the tax code. I talked earlier about the government suing itself at our expense, and perhaps the I.R.S. deserves the blame they receive, but I would think that the legislature had to read (maybe some small portion) and approve the code before it could be enacted and enforced. A comedian had a line that went "There is only one question on the tax form, How much did you make? After you answer that question the instructions were to "Send it in." The very size of the tax code tells you that it is wrong. The code deals with only one thing, income or lack thereof. For more than half of the existence of the U.S. Government, it did not rely on income tax.

In any case, I think we should know how much of the tax money collected does the I.R.S. spend on itself. In other words, how much does it cost to collect our taxes? The government should tell us. How many manhours went into drafting the code at our expense. When you have a lot of money and are required to pay a lot of taxes, you hire an accountant and a tax lawyer, both of which are tax deductible. The tax code, like most things that the government writes to control our lives, is convoluted and defies logic. When you are told to take percentages of this and add them to some other number and then divide by the square root of 13.67 and multiply by .00345 and when you complete this complex task it ends up being six percent, you know somebody is playing with your head.

The universal sales tax sounds interesting. The candidate that put it forth concluded that there is a hidden economy. This is made up of illegals, criminals and tax cheats. They pay nothing. If there was a tax on everything purchased, we would get some of that money. More than that though, it sounds simple and easy to police. Every retailer would collect the tax. Any wholesaler selling to anyone beside a retailer would be severely punished. The retailer would compute the gross sales and send a percentage to the government. We would all benefit from the person who feels the need to engage in conspicuous consumption. Hopefully, when all of the people working for the I.R.S. get laid off, the savings will spark the economy enough to find jobs for them all in retail.

I always like doing math problems. When I go to the gym I divide my repetitions into fractions and I know when I have completed 1/6th ,¼, 1/3rd , and so forth. However, I get lost when I try to compute my tax burden. I pay income tax to the federal government, the state government, and the local government. I pay tax on my phone bill, my gas bill, my electric bill. I pay tax on the gas for my car. I pay sales tax. I pay real estate school tax and real estate local tax. I know there must be more. And I just thought of it, capital gains tax. Wouldn't it be nice to have capital gains? You know what I mean, buy something and then later sell it for a profit. It would be like earning money and we have to pay tax on that. Well, it is not that simple.

Assume that I bought a 1953 Chevrolet Corvette for four thousand dollars in 1953. Assume that I sold it in 2008. I would pay capital gains tax on whatever I received for the car over four thousand dollars. In 1953 I was in my first year of high school. A loaf of bread was a nickel. Gas was less than twenty cents a gallon. Most people didn't make four thousand dollars a year. Today the average wage is probably in the fifty thousand dollar range. But if I sold my Corvette for fifty thousand, the forty six thousand more than I paid for it would be profit, and I would have to pay tax on it. If you have ten thousand in the bank and the inflation rate is four percent and you earn three percent on your money you have suffered a loss of one percent. Yet you must pay tax on the three percent you "earned." The last example, if you bought a house in 1950 for $8,000.00 and sold it in 2008 for $150,000.00 and moved to another similar home and paid $150,000 for the property, how would you realize a capital gain? You wouldn't, the money would be worth less. In that circumstance you would be allowed to carry the capital gain into the next property, meaning that your basis in the new house would be $8,000.00. Later on you might get to claim a one-time write off of some amount of the capital gains. But why? You really haven't made any money at all. It's a scam.

When you buy a product of any kind, you are paying tax on the purchase price other than sales tax. The product was delivered to the retailer in a truck or train that used fuel and the fuel was taxed. The people operating the truck or train were taxed on their income. The cost of transportation, including the taxes, are computed into the price. The product was made or packaged by someone who is paying income tax and that is included in the price. The raw material going into the product was collected by someone and shipped to the manufacturer, which is added to the price including all taxes at that level. There is no sales tax at the state level where I live on food stuffs bought in a supermarket. Food prepared for take-out is taxed. I eat them both. The food stuffs price, however, includes the tax paid to growers, preparers, shippers and the like.

Reading the foregoing you can understand how I could not figure out how much of the money I earn goes to taxes. It has been suggested that some number like forty percent of our income is paid in taxes. Others have said that there is a date sometime in April or May when we have reached the point that we have earned enough to pay all of our taxes for the year. I wish I could vacation until that day.

Racism & Race Relations

I recently read a letter to the opinion page of my local paper that was apparently written by an African American woman. She wrote that in her opinion the United States should apologize to all African Americans because we engaged in slavery of the African American people.

While I agree that slavery of any kind is reprehensible, it is certainly not exclusive to the African Americans. Webster defines slavery as "the state of a person who is chattel of another." Said another way, it can be defined as someone who is owned or the property of another. From a legal standpoint, slavery was abolished one hundred and fifty years ago, give or take a few years. The government was able to make it illegal to own another person and/or sell another person, but by no means was slavery abolished. There are any number of people currently in the United States who, for lack of a better definition, are slaves. Two quick examples could be Asians who are brought to United States illegally and then put to work for someone who has total control of the person until such time as the debt of the one controlled is paid in full. The debt is rarely paid in full since the controller sets the interest rate. The person controlled speaks little English, and can not strike out on their own, since they are illegal. Another example is the home aid person brought in from another country as a nanny or maid. They are totally controlled and dominated by the person who paid their way to the United States. I am certain that there many more of examples of people currently in the United States who could be defined as slaves.

This is by no means meant to diminish the horrible treatment of African Americans by other Americans who for one reason or another like to feel that there is someone lower in the pecking order than themselves. On the other hand, it should be recognized by everyone that even during the period that slavery was okay with the government, it was not okay with a huge number of people in the United States. When slavery was abolished many people in the United States were delighted. That does not mean that everyone started to share their Sunday dinner with the African American family who lived across town. Others who came to the United States through the early to middle 1900s were not treated better than the African Americans. Italians and Irish were certainly not welcomed with open arms by the Anglo Saxons who controlled most of the commercial enterprise. It was, however, easier for the new Americans to assimilate once they were here because they were, for the most part, unidentifiable from the Anglo Saxons once they learned the language. The assimilation, however, was not in every instance complete.

In Philadelphia as in many other cities where the immigrant populations came to seek employment and housing, the nationalities congregated in sections of the city. There were enclaves of Polish, Italians, Irish, Germans and Jews to cite a non exclusive list. To some extent the principle still exists today with the new enclaves of Russians, Indians, Spanish and others congregating with those of similar heritage.

However, as the years have passed many of the original enclaves of nationalities have diminished. In Philadelphia, South Philadelphia was the place to live if you were Italian. There were Italians in Philadelphia who did not speak English, despite the fact that they had lived in the United States for all of their adult lives. Similarly there were more than a handful of Polish people who spoke only Polish after spending 30 to 40 years living in the Bridesburg section of Philadelphia. Philadelphia also had Jewish neighborhoods, German neighborhoods and there were Black neighborhoods. For better or worse people wanted to live with people like themselves. Today it doesn't matter so much. Today you don't talk to your neighbor. Your children don't go out to play. Children play in the house on the computer or they are involved in organized and supervised play. My grandchildren are involved in soccer, baseball and gymnastics. They go to birthday parties at someone's house or a commercial establishment that is made for such an event.

Race and National origin still matter. Black people still want to feel accepted by everyone else, but they do not accept everyone else. Fifty years ago I enlisted in the Navy. I bunked in the Engineering quarters. There were machinist mates, boiler men and electricians. I can't remember the numbers but we were integrated. On the ship we were all friends and fellow workers, but when we went ashore in the United States, the White guys went to the White part of town and the Black guys went to the Black part of town.

When I came home from the Navy and joined the Police Department, I worked in the Black part of the city. I noticed a few things about the culture of the African American of the early to middle sixties. The first thing I noticed was that the African Americans wanted to be different. First, especially amongst the younger people the language was significantly different. Black teens coined words that had special meaning to them and were not meant for White people to understand. While the Black kids spoke English they spoke in a way that made the words difficult to understand. They wanted to be different and they wanted White people to feel excluded. While I sometimes saw Black people come to the section of the city in which I lived, I never, with the exception of business people who came to open their stores and conduct business, saw White people go into the Black neighborhood to shop or socialize. I patrolled the neighborhood and could sense a tension amongst the few Whites who were actually there and could also sense a barely controlled dislike for the White people who came to do business in the neighborhood. When riots occurred in 1964 many of the business properties were looted and damaged. The damage occurred to the stores owned by White people but rarely to those owned by Black business people.

Today young Black men wear there pants below the cheeks of their rear end. The underwear is visible to anyone passing them. Some young White men are dressing in the same fashion. It has been around for some time and seems to this observer to be on the wane. It is an attempt to be different in a way that is outrageous. Some misguided local legislators are attempting to make the fashion statement against the law. In doing so, in my opinion they are acknowledging the success of the fashion statement to make them stand out. Negative attention is still attention.

When I was growing up I went out the front door and played with the other kids in the neighborhood. By the age of 9 or 10 I would walk all over the neighborhood with my friends. We would go to the playground and choose up sides for baseball. We would play stick ball, wire ball, hide and seek, and always we would end up sitting on the front steps of someone's house until dinner time. My mother would tell me to go out and play. Usually that order was after I had completed some task around the house or yard. Nothing bad ever happened to me or any of my friends while we were outside playing. We were, depending on definition, either respectful or afraid of all adults. We were not afraid they would hurt us, but afraid they would tell our parents that we had done something bad.

Today parents don't accept the word of an adult relative to their children. Teachers, coaches, scout leaders, church leaders, and many others are all suspect. They may have other than wholesome motivation. Parents yell at teachers because their child is not doing well in school. Everyone except the parent is responsible for the failure of their child. At the same time it is unacceptable behavior for a parent to discipline their children in public, and to some extent in private. Children are advised that if they are being mistreated they should report their parents to the authorities. It should seem obvious that we have lost our direction. Discipline is necessary for every adult endeavor. Employment requires discipline. Driving a car requires discipline. How do our children learn discipline? Maybe the Purple Dinosaur is more capable of training our children than we are, but if so, we are at a bad point in human development.

Often times our government has taken the position that discipline is unattainable without the assistance of the government. They try to legislate a solution for every problem. The government even legislates a solution to a proposed problem. We now have crimes that are designated as hate crimes. The application of this legislation is to increase the severity of the crime if it appears to have been brought on by the perpetrator as a result of his/her dislike for the other person's racial heritage or religious leaning. In reality, it is a means to increase the penalty for any crime committed by a white person against a person of color. I don't profess to state this as an absolute certainty, but only as an observation. The only time that I see in the newspapers in the area, a report of someone being charged in a hate crime the perpetrator is White and the victim is Black. Why is it not a hate crime if the perpetrator is Black and the victim is White or Asian. Does the Black perpetrator not realize that the person who is their victim is a member of a race other than themselves? Is not the act of committing a crime against someone at least an implication of strong dislike?

Recently in the news, there were reports of statements made by a minister in the church that a presidential candidate attended. The statements condemned White people and the government. This particular minister had a huge congregation. It would seem to lead one to the conclusion that those people who were in the congregation either agreed, or did not strongly disagree with the statements of the minister. Are those types of statements leading us as a nation into a place where race, ethnicity, religion, sexual orientation, height, weight, physical attractiveness and assorted other differences don't matter? I think not. However, anyone who thinks they don't currently matter is living in a cave. Everything else aside, the advantage goes to the attractive person. For better or worse, an attractive person always has the advantage in every situation. Obtaining employment, getting raises, promotions, etc. are easier for the attractive person. It is known by anyone who surveys matters such as these that tall people also have an advantage. Heavy people suffer a disadvantage. These things are statistically true. What is not studied is preferential treatment. When Philadelphia Mayor John Street was sworn into office he was heard to say, the Brothers and the Sisters are now in charge. Many of the upper level positions went to Black people. No one complained openly about the hiring or appointment practices of the new mayor. Many of the insiders acknowledged that since a Black man was elected it was obviously their turn. The point is though, that when the Black man had a chance to show that he would be different than the White guys that preceded him, he didn't jump at the chance.

We really are more alike than we are different. John Kennedy appointed his brother to be Attorney General. Do you think it had anything to do with the fact that he was his brother? Patronage jobs go to cousins, uncles, friends and so on. Are they the most qualified? When I came out of the Navy, I tried to get information concerning the Plumber's Union. I was told that I needed to have a relative in the Union sponsor me. Human nature is hard to change. If we really were trying to change, we could start by outlawing any reference at all to a person's race or ethnicity on any form or application. Or we could say that if you are a citizen of the United States you could only be addressed as an American. Being an Italian American, Irish American, Polish American, African American, or Hispanic American would be against the law. Private clubs could only be made up of Americans, ergo there could be no Polish American String Band, no Italian restaurants. The secret handshake of the Mason's, or the wink and nod of the Sons of Italy would be forbidden under the law and no one could make a negative reference to any other American. A half step toward this type of unanimity could be that anyone professing to be an African American would have to be 100% African living in America. Where this could apply might be in those places where a racial preference is necessary. For example, if someone were seeking admission to a law school and did not score high enough in LSAT exam, they could fill one of the seats held aside for a minority person. If that minority was African American, they should show that they are 100% African American. Better yet, we could skip it all and admit that we are all prejudice.

Every decision we make in life is based to some degree upon prejudice. Sales people are more aware of this than anyone else. Politicians talk about it all the time. Appeal to the Black vote, appeal to the woman's vote, the elder vote, etc. We all look to our own well being in selecting a candidate. Who is going to treat us best first? It's all a little demeaning, but true. African Americans voted in a ninety percent plurality for the recent Black Presidential Candidate. White people whose vote was not about saying that they were erudite and intelligent voted for the White woman. The erudite voted for the Black man because they were showing that they were not going to be swayed by Race.

What's the solution? Acknowledge that prejudice exists. How can we not confuse ourselves when we continue to act dumb about the fact that attractive people fair better than unattractive people. Men are attracted to beautiful women and women are attracted to handsome men. Sure you can point to the occasional rich ugly goober who gets the beautiful woman, but he wouldn't be so lucky if she could land a rich good looking guy. Is it fair that someone who grows to be six feet ten inches should make a fortune playing basketball? Basketball discriminates against short people. Most professional sports are not racially and ethnically balanced. Professional Football teams do not represent the racial and ethnic make up of the nation as a whole.

Does anyone ever ask the question, why don't White parents want to send their children to a school whose students are predominately African American children? Or conversely, what is wrong with African American children attending a predominately African American school? How about, why don't good seasoned teachers want to teach in a predominately African American school? Is there anyone out there that doesn't know the real answer to these questions? We wrap ourselves in politically correct speech and ignore the problem. The problem is we cannot tell the truth. Even Black people cannot tell the truth without be accused of selling out or some other personal attack.

Politicians like to say that all politics is local. Society's problems are familial. We have to recognize that the failure of family structure is the major societal problem of this age. Neither teachers, police nor government can replace the strength of a strong family relationship. A weak family structure can be influenced by a strong family simply by being in the same area and knowing the strong family . When I was child there were small families and large families, there were those who had problems with alcohol and temper. The example set by a good strong family pulled on all of the others as an example to follow, a goal to seek, and most of all a happiness and contentment to envy and desire.

Today the path to easy street seems to be wealth without work, success without discipline, happiness and contentment without contribution. Sex, drugs and lawlessness are all efforts towards happiness. The effort is thoughtless and lacking in common sense. A sexual relationship is not a committed relationship. Years ago, a farmer wanted a woman who was strong and could help around the farm. She could also help by bearing good strong children who could help to grow the farm and ultimately operate the farm. The two would work as team toward a goal. Probably doesn't sound very romantic. On the other hand, a relationship built upon sexual attractiveness is by definition doomed to fail. Few people remain sexually attractive for their entire life. If sexual attractiveness is the sole reason for being drawn to a person, hopefully other qualities will emerge to allow a true balanced relationship to grow. Unfortunately, it usually doesn't, which leads to the statistic that over 50% of marriages fail. Hidden along side that failure is the number of people who do not get married when they have sex and the reward of the sexual relationship is a child. So, not only are the children of failed marriages at risk, but huge numbers of children born out of wedlock are also at risk.

As a lawyer I have seen parents who put the interest of their children ahead of the interest of themselves. When a couple is that reasonable and mature, I generally wonder why the parties are divorcing. While everyone knows a woman, and more rarely a man, who can provide all of the parental services necessary for raising a child to be mentally strong and physically healthy, no one would argue that two caring and mentally mature parents is a superior combination. More on this subject later. The point I am trying to make is that in African American communities there are many more children at risk. There are more children who grow up without a strong joint effort to raise them. In some cases children are being raised by grandmothers whose children were raised without the contribution of a loving father. I have been around African Americans my entire adult life. When I was young we lived separately. When I was a late teenager and in the Navy, Black people could not sit in the front of the bus down south, nor could they drink water from the same fountain that White People drank from. The latter 1950s and early 1960s brought about many changes. Not all of the changes yielded the result of a better society.

The poor treatment of Blacks by the government (not necessarily by the people) was unsupportable. African Americans are in every way the equal of White people and in some cases superior. Jimmy the Greek was fired for stating the obvious, that Black men are usually superior in athletics to White men. If that isn't true then please explain the imbalance on sports teams. How can 20% of the population make up 98% of the professional basketball players and by all appearances over 75% of the professional football players. But athletics aside, African Americans can excel in scholastics. There are innumerable Black scholars in all fields, medicine, economics, sciences, to name a few. The problem is that in proportion to the White population Blacks do not seem to gravitate toward the scholarly fields. The entertainment field and the sports field seem to draw the attention of young Black people and to a large degree they are proportionately more successful in both fields than White people. However, when the goal of a young Black person is to be successful in the field of sports and entertainment, they make no secondary plan. The chance of success is miniscule and the chance of failure is huge.

Why do young Black people not understand the huge chance of failure and make a secondary plan? I suspect it is because they are not grounded in a loving and caring family structure. When a child is raised in a neighbor riddled with crime and poverty role models are not found in the industries. The drug dealer, the gang leader, the neighborhood tough guy, and other unsavory characters are the people who the youngster sees and must deal with on a daily basis. When the road is not smooth and the path not effortless, the immature and ungrounded person looks around for a scapegoat to blame for failure. White kids go home and tell their parents that the teacher hates them. Black kids internalize the feeling that they cannot succeed because they are Black. The Black community leaders compound the feeling that a Black child cannot succeed because White people (the government) do not treat everyone (Blacks) equal and do not provide equal opportunities. The statistics bear out the conclusions because for the most part schools in Black neighborhoods do not have the same scholastic standards that White neighborhood schools have. Moving the Black children to the White neighborhood schools works to a limited degree, until the schools have a large percentage of Black ungrounded and immature students who create the same non-learning environment that existed in the Black neighborhood school.

What's the solution? Stop kidding ourselves. For the most part, bad children make bad adults. At some point in the future, if the population continues to grow at the current rate, we will take steps to control population or starve to death. Certainly, with the modernization of farming and the scientific manner in which food can be produced it might take some time, but we are heading there. What might happen is that somehow people will be reversibly sterilized at birth. In order to have children, a person would need to attend parenting classes, which would include nutrition, child development, and also provide a satisfactory response to the issue of the responsibility that they were undertaking. Once that was completed the sterilization would be reversed and childbearing could occur. Before you start laughing or slapping your head in incredulity give a minute's thought. We license drivers because the act of driving an automobile is a dangerous and costly thing. Innocent people could get hurt or killed by the bad driver. How much do we, as the taxpaying public, pay for the care of unwanted and undisciplined children. How many people are hurt by the actions of the undisciplined. In school they disrupt the class and cause the learning cycle for the other children to come to a halt. In the halls they harass and intimidate the children who are simply in school to learn. They change the atmosphere to one that becomes unsusceptible to learning. When they drop out of school they are juvenile delinquents and when they become adults they are criminals. In those instances, we the taxpaying public, pay for the Police, the Courts and the Prisons, and are also burdened with the cost of taking care of the victims of the undisciplined's behavior.

Am I referring to Black children? Yes and no. Yes, Black children can be undisciplined and may account for a larger percentage of undisciplined children and undisciplined adults than they are a percentage of the population. But they are by no means the only people who bear unwanted children. For the moment, however, that pie in the sky solution is unavailable. Church leaders, Politicians, and probably a huge majority of the population would believe such a thing to be heresy. The common sense of requiring a license to have children almost seems Chinese. Common sense does not always prevail.

The alternative is to speak to the issue. Speak the truth. Not the politically correct statement, but the truth. The errant parents of undisciplined children should be castigated for their lack of citizenship. They are contributing to the worsening of the economy, the lessening of the quality of life for their neighbors, and the loss of learning environment for the other children in the neighborhood.

We cannot look to the government to solve this problem. Think back, has the government ever solved a problem? Some of the recipients of the largess of the other taxpayers have made a success of their lives, but at what cost? It has been shown that welfare created fatherless homes. When the poor could not collect welfare because there was a man living in the home, the man left, except to return to create more fatherless children. Everyone can point to the rare mother who knew what she was doing and instilled values and civility in her children. She would have probably done it without welfare. The government should not take credit for it. Truth be told, welfare was a program that like most programs serves a political ulterior motive. The motivation is to increase power, (vote getting) or increase influence (creating government jobs and bureaucracy) or increase wealth, politicians do not act altruistically. Even when a politician said we are going to cure cancer in this century, which hasn't happened, although inroads have been made, he was not saying that someone in government was going to find the cure. What he was saying was that we (the government) are going to give huge sums of money to medical facilities of which we know nothing, but are located in favorable districts and therefore will create jobs in those areas. What happens then? Jobs create a favorable economic climate which in turn creates wealth, which in turn leads to political contributions to the legislator who brought home the bacon.

No. This solution must come from the grass roots. The people who feel slighted must stop it. Look around. Ask the short man if he feels that he has been overlooked for promotion. Ask the Italian if he has ever felt discriminated against. And on and on. We have all been discriminated against. Blacks discriminate against other Blacks and against other people when they are in power. Many times I listened to arguments amongst African Americans while on patrol in the Police Department. Like every other person on the globe, they can be verbally brutal when angry. The slurs are fast and furious during verbal altercations. Oddly, African Americans are the only people who are allowed to say certain words today. How fair is that? As I stated earlier, when a Black mayor was elected in Philadelphia there was certainly reverse discrimination. Maybe your grandfather and grandmother had reasons to be angry, but you need to get over it. Someone once said the best revenge is success. However, if revenge is the motivation success is going to be hard to find. Determination to succeed is a positive motivation that cannot be deterred by a small minded person who might place themselves in the way. Becoming a productive and law abiding citizen with positive motivation is not being an "Uncle Tom."

We must all recognize that having children is a responsibility, an honor, a pleasure (when done right) and extremely rewarding (when done right). Having sex without thinking about the resulting child is criminal to the child. Knowing that you are the result of a one night stand, that the person who fathered you did not think enough of your mother to leave his name, that your mother was ill-prepared to take on the responsibilities of motherhood, in most instances would not lead the child to think highly of himself. It is not hard to understand why such children are overwhelmed with negativity. The government cannot face up to spending all of the social security money, how can they help us out of this situation? They can't. We must do it ourselves. Think and speak out. Demand discipline. Don't be so forgiving and unconscious regarding moral judgment and general good judgment. Be supportive of the local school district and take part.

EDUCATION

I went to grade school in the 1940s and early 1950s. I finished high school and went into the Navy in 1957. I joined the Police department in 1961 and went to night college from 1966 until I graduated Law school in 1983. My college degrees are a Bachelor in Science (Business Administration), A Master's (Public Administration) and a Law Degree. In addition to the formal education, I also either taught myself or learned through watching others, to do home repairs, construction, auto repairs, electrical repairs, cement work, bricklaying, ceramic tile installation, plumbing and many more. At this point in my life I am in concert with the Pennsylvania Dutch saying, "Ve get too soon old and too late shmart." I would have enjoyed being able to do all of the things that I can now do when I was in my twenties and thirties

Education is a great deal more than going to school. I can remember a number of people outside of my family who had an impact on my life. I responded to some of my teachers and even after 50 years I still remember a few and the help that they gave to me. Some of the help may have been through observation of the manner in which they handled things. Some may have been through one on one communication. While in the Navy, I worked for a man who supervised the engine room, and I recall with gratitude the profound impact that he had on my life. I know that during my time in the Police Department, I was considered by those that worked for me, a good supervisor. I was, through self awareness, cognizant that in certain important respects I was, in fact, a good supervisor. I owe a great deal to the man I worked for in the engine room for my success in the Police Department. It is important to point out here that he was not working with a rock, but with a piece of clay. I was eager to learn and willing to listen and think.

It was not always that way. During my high school years, I was not a stellar student, simply because I had too many other things on my mind. In grade school I was more closely supervised and even disciplined. Philadelphia Public school teachers of the 1950s would pull hair and crack knuckles with a ruler among other disciplinary actions such as sitting in the corner and writing on the blackboard. My parents were not violent people, however, they practiced mild physical discipline. They were not the least bit concerned about a teacher pulling my hair to insure that I was attentive in class. I am sure that had I come home with a bruise or a cut or some like evidence of discipline over the top, they would have had questions for the teacher. For the most part, however, none of us would go home and complain about being disciplined because it would likely have resulted in more discipline.

The education that was stressed in my school years can best be described as the three Rs. That stands for reading, writing and arithmetic. I believe that the educational system has departed from the emphasis on those three subjects. I am typing this on a computer that has spell and punctuation check. I use calculators in my office and at home for some of the math problems that I face. I also watch television where a novel made into a movie is available. However, composing a readable paper is very important to a lawyer who often has to argue through written words the fine points of law and the persuasive reasoning to apply those laws or not apply them to the situation involving a client. I must be able to read and understand law books. Arithmetic is part of budgeting, shopping, business and everyday living. I deliberately forgo the use of a calculator from time to time to insure that I have not lost my edge. I read novels constantly for enjoyment. All of the above are the reasons for my success in finishing my post high school education. Through the years I have taken on a project after project that made me grateful to my teachers and my parents for instilling in me the love of reading. My parents encouraged me to pick something that I liked and read it for enjoyment. As a youngster I read many books about the sea. Pirate stories, Moby Dick and the like were my initial foray into reading and soon I found detective stories and comedies to my liking.

About twenty years ago I constructed a kit car. It was a replica of a 1952 MGTD. The car was made of fiberglass and was installed over a Volkswagon "Beetle" chassis. The kit came with an instruction manual that started with opening the box and ended with starting the car. I was very proud when the vehicle passed Pennsylvania State Inspection and declared roadworthy. Carefully reading the instructions and following them made success at this project achievable.

Another thing stressed during my schooling was citizenship. Patriotism was a matter of great importance to my teachers. It still is to me to this day. During the 1960s when I began to attend college, many of the professors and instructors were not so patriotic. They associated an unpopular war with their lack of love or dislike of our country. It was not uncommon for college students, with the encouragement of the instructors in the institutions, to engage in activity that could only be described as criminal. Today, we are again engaged in an unpopular war, but the public has rightly directed their angst at the politicians and not the soldiers who are simply following orders. From my perspective, the activities of the sixties were the turning point from what had been a fine educational system to one that is permeated with activists. The educators of the sixties influenced the college students who became the teachers and professors of the seventies and have led to a loss of discipline at the teaching level as well as the student level.

I remember one incident that occurred in the later 1960s or early 1970s. I had taken a day course in composition that was unavailable to me at night. I was at the time about thirty years old. The day class was made up of people one or two years out of high school. The instructor was a young woman, no older than me, who wore bush outfits to class like she was headed for a safari. She smoked cigars the size of a king-sized cigarette in class and carried a thermos bottle. She would pour the contents into an opaque cup so that the class could not determine what she was actually drinking. The class, with the exception of me (it seemed) thought that she was really cool. The nature of the subject was English II which was grammar. The instructor assigned us to read stories written by existentialist writers and then write reports on the stories. When I received a C for my efforts, I reviewed the paper and found no carets throughout the paper indicating grammatical errors or misspellings. I questioned the instructor and the ensuing argument became heated to the chagrin of the rest of the class. I argued that the paper was miss-marked. She argued that I missed the point of the writing. She had converted the course to suit her own predetermined belief and was using the class as a forum to extend her beliefs. None of my teachers in grade school or high school would have done anything similar.

A teacher is in control of other people. Being in control is a huge responsibility. When I was supervisor in the Police Department I recognized that some of the people who worked for me felt that I was the font of all wisdom. Some of the people who worked for me wanted me to think that they thought I was the font of all wisdom. Being a good supervisor is the knowledge that there are both types of people and that neither is necessarily a good thing.

I have always been of the impression that school was intended to teach a person how to learn. Solving a math problem is instruction in the manner of life. We are told to examine the different elements of the problem to see how they relate to each other and then by using certain rules, solve the problem. Writing, or said another way, grammar, is the method of proper communication with other people. If we seek information from someone, it is desired to properly state the question so that the question is properly understood and the person can then provide the appropriate answer. Similarly, if information is properly sought from us, we can answer the question. We must be careful to insure that the message we send is the message received. Using proper grammar is paramount to being understood.

Reading is quite obviously the method whereby we are enabled to expand on our own our learning potential. If we read and understand, our learning potential is boundless. In other courses that I took in grammar school and in high school, such as science, I was shown how the application of the skills I had acquired in the three Rs made scientific learning obtainable.

Today, I feel that we are abandoning the principle of teaching someone how to learn in favor of teaching what has been learned. Computer technology is a wonderful thing. The information available to people can be not only instantaneous, but boundless. The problem is, in my mind, that the foundation is not laid by good basic schooling so that the information found can be properly evaluated and cataloged by an individual. Young children are at risk on the computer, not just to predators, but also to information overload. The feeling that the computer is the answer to every problem eliminates the need for developing skills of discernment in the individual.

Sometime soon, we will come to realize that the computer, like many other things that we use, consume, or deal with daily, must be carefully used to avoid calamity. Salt is a wonderful enhancement to food. We all know, however, that too much salt can be harmful, and in great excess, fatal. Water can kill not only by drowning, but by over hydration. We need the Suns rays for vitamin D, but excessively it can cause skin cancer and death. The computer has become an all purpose substitute for entertainment, communication and study. A type of shorthand language has developed for computer and text message communication. While it is functional for its purpose, when a person spends too much time on the computer, the shorthand can create a dysfunction in normal writing and speaking skills. When I was child we had no such devices. I think that even if we had, I would have considered sitting inside the house for hours a severe punishment. There are some scholars who feel that an important part of childhood is being lost when children are not encouraged to go outside to play. Take a walk through the woods, go down to the creek and look for snakes, minnows and frogs.

Educating the youth of our country is the most important task that our country faces today. We rely on the youths of today to be the Soldiers and Sailors, Marines and Air Force that protect us from foreign invaders. They must become the Police and Firefighters, Border Guards and Coast Guard who protect us at home. We ask our youth to sacrifice their very lives to be our protectors. Our youth also become the medical people who take care of us when we are ill. The new age farmers who supply us with food and very importantly, they become the parents who are raising the next generation.

Does anyone stop and reflect back on their youth and recall what their parents contributed to their maturity and abilities? I certainly do. My parents were not perfect, but they both cared. Both in their own way wanted nothing but the best for my sister and me. They advised and disciplined and provided a wholesome life. It wasn't Leave it to Beaver, but it wasn't bad. I learned from their mistakes as much as from the things they did right. A fellow I grew up with said to me that he couldn't get over how smart his father had become while he was away in the Army. When he was a teenager his father was about the dumbest guy around. When he was twenty-two and sat home and talked about life with his dad, he was dumbfounded by the change. He said it tongue-in-cheek, because the change was in him. He became mature enough to appreciate his father. Sometimes the things we learn are not instantly appreciated. A good teacher should not be looking for the light bulb to go off over everybody's head when they stand before the class and impart wisdom. Sometimes it takes awhile.

The important part of all this is not necessarily about the content of the lesson, but about the quality of the person providing the lesson. I am sure that my parents loved me and I am sure that my grammar school and high school teachers were devoted to their jobs. If they had ulterior motivation it was never apparent to me. During my college years I recognized plenty of instructors who were more interested in self aggrandizement than the absorption of knowledge by the students. Unfortunately, for the younger students, they were not as grounded as I from being in the Navy and the Police Department to have the strength and maturity to filter through the puff to find the kernel.

Our institutional educational systems must be fashioned to teach children to become productive adults. Today, as I stated earlier, families are in distress. They aren't families. Children are not being raised by their mothers and fathers, but by mothers and step-fathers, or mothers and uncle Harry or just Bill. Since the Second World War when moms left the house to go to work, many have remained at jobs to the detriment of family life. Before your cheeks get red, there are plenty of women who are capable of handling a job and a family and the resulting children grow into fine adults. In some cases the women raise families without the aid of a male partner to help raise and support the children. The problem is that many women are not capable of handling the stress of raising children and keeping a job with limited education and limited job skills. Unfortunately, these seem to be the women that bear the most children. The children that result from those situations are at risk. Some may turn out just fine, but many will not. Those that are not will be the ones that bear the most children. Without taking draconian measures regarding reproduction, we are left with only the choice of attempting to reach some of those at-risk children. We must first acknowledge the problem and then take steps to remedy the problem as best that we can. Stopping the cycle of a bad child, bad adult and bad parent being one in the same over the years.

The first step is to carefully, statistically register each child with information gleaned from the parent or guardian. Those children who are statistically at risk must be taught life lessons as well as school lessons. Homemaking, nutrition, health, childcare should be filtered into their education. Even non-at-risk children could benefit from the lessons. Obesity is rampant in our society and brought on by a variety of causes, but some of the more apparent are no structured meal program and no exercise. By structured meal program I'm talking about breakfast and dinner at home with a prepared meal of some type. My family always ate breakfast at home. Nothing fancy, just cereal and fruit, maybe toast and juice. My dad was a pharmacist so we took our share of vitamins. Back in the ancient times of youth, when I had a job during the summer, my mother made me a lunch to take to work. Dinner was at home. Dinners included some vegetables, which at the time I thought I hated, potatoes and meat. We did not deprive ourselves of desserts. Neither my mom, dad nor my sister or me were skinny, but we were not obese.

Today, in addition to the loss of nutritional value from a breakfast and dinner at home, the loss of camaraderie is another deficit in childhood development. It could be argued that our educational system should not be burdened with replacing the function of parents, but, if we are to properly train the replacements for ourselves, we must face reality. We must address the total lack of guidance that should come from parents. Perhaps it was lost to the parents' generation. If so, parents would not have the knowledge that would enable them to instruct their children in proper nutrition.

During my life in the Police Department, I would work shift work. This would mean that over the span of a month, I would work midnight to 8 AM, 8 AM till 4 PM and 4 PM to midnight. I would see kids on their way to school, men and women on their way to work. In the poorer neighborhoods, it seems that the kids would not eat at home, but would have cake or a doughnut and a soda for breakfast. Why I noticed was because early on in my Police life, I became a father and I knew the cost of eating from the fast food or sweets aisle. Making my son eat breakfast at home was not only more nutritional but also less expensive.

If we examine everything in its simplest form and simplest language I think we would resolve more of the seemingly difficult dilemmas facing us today. For example, our forefathers set about establishing the government to serve us. Today the government serves itself. Ask yourself why do we need a government? The first and simplest response is that we need to organize to protect ourselves from foreign countries who might want to do us harm. We seem to take on the responsibility cloak whenever there is harm to anyone anywhere, but our first responsibility should be to those of us in our own country. The second response should be that we need to organize to protect us from people who are just like us and live in this country. It is there that we open Pandora's Box. Do we need Police protection from criminals? Or, do we need protection from bad business dealings, polluters, profiteers, sickness, bad financial choices of our own, bad safety habits of our own, lack of saving for the future, poor retirement planning, failure to obtain marketable skills to enable us to make a satisfactory wage, and on and on.

Well, one thing that we have recognized is an obligation to educate our children. The government has assumed the responsibility. The failure of the system to educate properly has led to an undereducated workforce. The failure of the family to educate has led to overcrowded prisons, a 50%+ divorce rate, at risk children in every community, unhealthy children and adults, a multitude of children being born to unwed mothers who are unable or unwilling to accept the mantle of parenting. The expense of failing to educate is far worse than the cost of properly educating.

Failing to educate one person who then either fathers a child or bears a child who is unwanted costs the rest of society a great deal. Without examining the harm that the unwanted child will suffer, look to the cost to society of taking care of the unwanted child. The prisons are full of unwanted children who have reached adulthood. Many of the people being treated in hospitals are being paid for by taxpayers because they have no job or the job they have is not worthy of health insurance. Surely, it can be said that genetics has a great deal more to do with whether we end up with heart disease or diabetes, and while it may be true it is a cop out. We need quality health education.

How do we get started when the system has deteriorated to such a degree? The first step is the hardest. Agree that schools require disciplined students and disciplined teachers. Students who disrupt others must be removed from the class. Boot camp tactics might be called for to remedy the situation. The parents of disruptive children must be advised and their cooperation sought. However, under no circumstances would parents be allowed to second guess the system. A parent who doesn't want their child in the system could remove them to some private school or home school, but under no circumstance would they or their attorneys disrupt the process. Teachers who have their own agendas should be asked to leave the system. Education worked in the 1940s, 1950s and 1960s. There were classes in catholic schools where a nun would have 50, 60 or more children in her class. She would teach them all because she maintained discipline. Parents might not agree with everything that the nun did, and the nun may have been wrong on occasion, but the children for the most part learned what they were supposed to learn. Philadelphia in the 1940s and 1950s had the highest rated schools and for the most part the best school system in the country. The major factor in my mind, having been there, was discipline. Discipline must come first and continue through senior high school. All of the other subjects will be easier to teach and learn when discipline is primary.

MARRIAGE AND DOMESTIC RELATIONS

During my tenure in the Police Department I was assigned to a district station house that had approximately two hundred and fifty officers assigned. I was in charge of twenty five percent of them. At the time there were only men in the district. Of the roughly sixty people assigned to my platoon, there were four or five who had never been married. There was another perhaps eight to ten who were married once and still making it work. The remaining forty five were separated, divorced, remarried, divorced again or some other form of dissolution of the marital relationship. My platoon was no different by any large degree than any of the other platoons in the district or the city. The only difference would have been in those areas where the new recruits were assigned. Once the officers had five or six years on the job the percentage of marital strife reached the norm.

While the situation may have been worse in the Police Department than in other professions, I am, through the experience of my second profession, sure that it was not much worse.

In Pennsylvania as in many other states, the divorce laws have changed to make getting a divorce much easier from a legal standpoint. Before the change, in the early 1980s, a divorce was only granted for cause. One party had to claim that the other party had been unfaithful, abusive, or some like infraction. In some cases the claims were pure fiction to which both parties agreed. After a hearing that only the claiming party appeared, the court would grant the requested divorce. Now if the parties agree that the marriage is broken, the court will grant a divorce. Some might argue that the change has brought about or caused the increase in the number of divorces. My perspective is different. I believe we are on a continuum that had led us to this point.

One of the beginning threads of the continuum was the Second World War. Men went into the armed services to fight for our country and women left the home and went to work. To some extent the women never went back. Now, to live in the style to which we think we have grown accustomed, and therefore have the right, requires two sources of income. Men and women spend more time at work with people of the opposite sex than they spend at home with their spouse. If both parties work the same shift and the same days, their mornings contain little quality time with each other. They are too busy getting up and getting ready to go to work. Late afternoon and early evening are spent with meal preparation and post meal clean up, leaving only a few hours of awake time to relate to each other. Weekends and holidays are spent shopping or pursuing individual goals or entertainment. If there are children, a great deal of the available time is spent tending to them. There is little time spent between the spouses alone.

The happy marriages recognize the goal, which is family unity and family growth. Part of that unity and growth is the health of the relationship between spouses. Parties who are centered in the marriage find that the small amount of alone time is actually sufficient time for the properly motivated. However, it is not enough time if the relationship has weaknesses. When two people work different shifts the problems multiply and magnify. The Police Department of my era changed shifts every eight days. The shifts went from midnight to eight AM for six out of eight days and then four to midnight for six out of eight days and finally eight AM to four PM for the final leg of the rotation for six out of eight days. If the Police Officer's spouse worked a steady shift it was difficult to have ten or twelve collective hours a month of good time together.

Another thread of the continuum is defining marriage roles. Roles in a marriage are not as easily defined as they were as little as seventy years ago. At that time a woman stayed at home and took care of the many functions of being a housewife and mother. She had her work cut out for her. If she was good at her job she made good meals and kept and cleaned house. Meals were important elements in the overall health and happiness of the family. When I was a child, there were very few if any prepared foods. The clothes washer was not automatic and we did not spin the clothes dry. We had to run the clothes through the ringer and hang them on the line. There were no clothes dryers. We peeled potatoes, snapped beans, and when the meal was over we washed and dried the dishes by hand. A wife in the era prior to the Second World War had a job in the home. Since that time so much of our lives have changed it almost seems unbelievable when I look back and think of the changes. It is easy to recognize the positive aspects of the changes. It is a great deal more difficult to see the negatives.

One of the negatives is that someone looking for a spouse doesn't know what to look for. Back in the day a woman looked for a good provider for a husband and a man looked for a wife who was not afraid to work in the home. Today both people work and earn so that they can afford all of the conspicuous consumption that advertising tells us is necessary. Obsolescence occurs today before a product is out of the box. We need the latest and the best, so there is a need to look for the next product, almost as soon as we begin to use the new one. Food requires no preparation and the laundry and the dishes almost wash themselves. So what should a person look for in a prospective spouse?

If we put the question to those people who are actually looking for a spouse, the answers could be all over the map but probably two would appear often. Sex appeal and earning capacity would probably rank very high in a survey. If someone was teaching a course in marriage preparation, I would suggest that required material for the course should include a movie from a long time ago called, "Lovers and other Strangers." The movie was comedy about the preparation and the marriage of the younger brother in an Italian family. The most memorable line in the movie is spoken by the wife of the older brother, Diane Keaton. She had just informed her in-laws that she and their son were getting a divorce. After a lengthy question and answer session the question of why did you get married in first place came up. Diane's reply was "because we looked good on the beach together and his hair smelled like raisins."

Probably the two most important decisions in life are made without careful thought and without any education. Marriage and children both occur to a large degree because of sex. Years ago I knew an Italian man who went back to Italy and selected the husband for his daughter. When I first found out I laughed and thought what a crazy thing to do. Upon reflection, though, it makes better sense than letting our libidos do it for us. The man loved his daughter very much and was extremely protective of her. The things that he looked for in a man for his daughter, were all of the lasting qualities that contribute to a marriage and give it a chance to last. He had to be able to provide for his daughter. He had to have the character that would insure that he would never mistreat his daughter. He had to be relatively healthly and of adequate looks. Certainly my friend did not want grotesque grandchildren. So he was cognizant of the traits and genes that were being passed to them. His decision was made coldly and calculatedly without the emotional element of infatuation. As far as I know the couple have remained married through the two or three decades since the marriage.

It wouldn't seem that we could ever go back to the time when our family would select the mate for us. So how do we get past this dilemma? Go back to the last chapter titled education and recognize that we must do something about the approaching adulthood of the students. Marriage, childbearing and rearing, should be mandatory subjects taught in school. Schools now give sex education classes. They demonstrate condoms by stretching them over a cucumber. They teach that families can be a man and a woman or a man and a man or a woman and a woman. But what about the choice of a mate and what about the responsibilities of each party to the bearing of a child and the rearing of a child? As far as I know the effort to help the burgeoning adults with the latter is absent.

In addition to viewing the movie I suggested above, I would suggest the familiarization of each student with a marriage contract. Just knowing about it would help many young adults to recognize what they are getting into and what they can expect to get out of a marriage. The marriage contract requires the parties to acknowledge their individual responsibilities in the union. While having someone to have sex with on a regular basis would seem to be enough to sustain a fifty or sixty year marriage, it isn't. Earlier on I said that a marriage based on sex appeal alone was doomed to failure. Without a great deal of luck, there is no question that the statement is true. A marriage contract lays out the responsibilities and allows the parties to see what is expected of them and what they should expect.

I have been a lawyer for about twenty five years. During that time my practice has morphed slowly into what it is today. It started with about 50 to 60 percent of my work being in the Domestic Relations field. Divorces, child support, custody, protection from abuse, equitable distribution and more. I was always amazed at the level of hatred that some people had for the soon to be ex-spouse. What could change so dramatically that a person you were willing to be naked in front of was now to be detested. I would sometimes ask the questions necessary for determining the issue of legal separation. One of the factors was that to be legally separated you could not engage in sexual relations. People could be legally separated and still live in the same house if they kept to themselves and did not sleep together. I would be surprised to learn that the parties had been in bed together only weeks before the appointment with me and still could display hatred and seek vengeance.

There were moments when I thought I could help people reconcile their differences and go on with their marriage. Exploration of the issue sometimes led to a dramatic change in the person who was sitting in my office. Having the need to put something into words and explain it logically to another person sometimes sheds light on the true severity of the issues at hand. There were times when I would recommend counseling. Other times I concluded that the parties did not get married for any of the right reasons and counseling would not help when the parties were not willing to contribute to the outcome.

Another part of my practice was business formation. I would discuss business formation with a client and often found that the business structure sought was a partnership and the client wanted me to protect him/her from making a bad decision. My advice was always the same, enter a partnership as though the partner is your enemy and you have a good chance of remaining friends. Enter a partnership as friends and there is good chance you will end up enemies. Why? Simply because we tend to think that we are on the same wave length with our friends. What is a day's work? Two friends might answer the question differently. Who is going to sweep the floor, open at eight AM, close at ten PM, carry the boxes, talk to the customers, count the money, all could yield different answers as could many other questions. All of the questions should be asked prior to committing money to a venture, no matter what the amount of money or the venture. When explained in that way the client generally wanted a fleshed out partnership agreement to control the business venture rather than a simple hand shake and giving over the check.

When you read the foregoing, you probably say, hey that makes sense, going into business with someone requires a great deal of care and examination. What about marriage? Putting $25,000 or $50,000 into a business is nothing when compared to marriage. From a money standpoint alone, every dime we make from the date of our marriage is marital property. More importantly, however, is failure. When the business fails you shut the door. You take your losses and you move on. When marriage fails, especially if there are children, the emotional price tag is huge. So why shouldn't people be better prepared for marriage.

Getting married and having children are two of the most important decisions that a person can make in their life and we leave it to some moron nineteen or twenty year old with a raging libido to conclude on their own with no help from anyone. As a parent I know that telling a twenty year old adult child that they are making a mistake is to insure that the mistake gets made. Parents theorize that by telling your son or daughter that you think their boyfriend or girlfriend is really nice and a quality person is enough to get rid of them. It may work in a rare instance but is probably a fallacy. The marriage choice should never be left to the last minute. We should be trained at an earlier age what marriage is about and especially what the addition of a child really means.

A friend of mine told me that his father suggested he should marry the girl who loves him and not the girl he loves. It sounds like a plan, but what if the girl's father told her the same thing. No, as cold and calculating as it may seem there must be an element of business in selecting a mate. Your idea of what marriage entails and whether your partner agrees, should not be left to be discovered subsequent to taking the vows. Nor should you think that living with someone prior to marriage is like a trial period. There is something about the permanence of marriage that is not present in the living arrangement. Some element of being on one's best behavior exists while living together. The knowledge that the trap has sprung after the marriage changes the parameters of the deal.

Considering the current status of longevity of marriage, it probably should not be left to parents to train the poor children by example. A constant stream of boyfriends and girlfriends after the parents have divorced is not a good training ground. Perhaps you might think that it would train children what not to do, but they probably don't understand enough about the marriage failure to have a good judgment of what went wrong. Then there is the knowledge of their parents physically and emotionally engaged with someone other than their other parent. This knowledge does not set the stage for mom and dad to explain the pitfalls of sleeping around.

Formal training seems to be the only recourse, teaching children the purpose of marriage and children as well as the responsibilities of both. The purpose of marriage is an illusive and most times unexplained phenomenon. In the 1950s when I was a teenager most girls wanted to go steady by 15 or 16 and be engaged by 18 or 19. Most of the boys ages 11 to 30 had no clue of their own. They knew they wanted to be in the company of girls, but probably could not explain why to anyone except another boy. This was because like most of the lesser species, boys wanted to mate. Also like most of the lesser species after they mated the boys wanted to leave the rest of the matter to the girls.

On the other side of the coin if you queried people who in later life felt that they had a good marriage, some might be at a loss to explain why. Being a man I can only give my point of view from one man's perspective. Men for the most part need to be and act manly. In a good relationship with a woman, a man can feel manly and the woman will accept his manliness without question. I also think the reverse is true.

In relationships with people of the same sex manliness or womanliness is not a given. Another man can challenge your manliness in any number of ways. Physically, intellectually, or socially, one man can reach to the top of the heap and gain recognition from other men and, much more desirably, from women. Being attractive to women scores high points with other men. Women are alike in that they compete for attention. Women's clothing with exposed cleavage and tight places to show curves, are meant not only to attract men, but also to intimidate other women. This is not unlike the mating rituals of animals.

The good relationship between a man and a woman recognizes the role that each must have in the relationship and develop a level of comfort and acceptance of their role and the role of the mate. This role acceptance should lead to a higher comfort level in the couple's relationship with people of the same sex outside of the marriage relationship. A man in a good relationship with his spouse, need not puff his chest out when in the presence of women as he no longer has the need or desire to mate outside of his relationship. The necessary ritual is only performed at home to a willing and appreciative mate.

This is not an effort to minimize in any way the relationship of two people in a good solid marriage. We are superior to the lesser species in a great many respects, although not all. That topic is a subject for another discussion. Suffice to say, two people can have a good solid relationship based on respect, mutual purpose, understanding and not just a willingness, but a desire to confront issues and ameliorate the problems that arise when opinions differ. In a good relationship people have differing opinions and are not compelled to change their opinion. Compromise is only necessary when it is absolutely necessary. When you need a car and one wants a black sedan and the other a white convertible and two cars are impossible a compromise must be struck. Differing tastes in food, music, art, reading material, politics can be topics for discussion but should not lead to upset. During a presidential election cycle it might be wise to not discuss at length the positives of your republican candidate if your mate is a democrat. Recognition of the greater good is a must. Winning an argument requires defeating the opposition. Defeat should never come at the cost of a good relationship.

Can this sort of thing be taught in a school setting to children of any age? Certainly. When I was in school we were taught citizenship. Not just citizenship in the state or the nation but citizenship in the neighborhood and the household. We were compelled to get along with our classmates. Problems were addressed, not swept under the table. One student would never be allowed to disrupt a class. The attention seekers of my time always got the attention, but it was attention meant to regain control of the class. We were constantly impressed with the purpose of our schooling and the benefit received by cooperation and the benefit lost by inattention. A good relationship is based on a mutuality of purpose. Cooperation leads to benefit and inattention to loss.

Times have changed and housekeeping is sometimes shared. Housekeeping tools and products have turned what took a housewife all of her waking hours to accomplish into short work. While I would never qualify as a gourmet, the sauces, dressings, seasonings, prepared main courses, vegetables are as good or better today, made in moments in a pot of boiling water or in the microwave, than anything my thirty I.Q. palate could devour in the 1950s when it was all made by hand.

I have always been a handyman. I learned to fix most everything in the home and garage long ago. Much of what I learned and the tools I used long ago are now passe. The tools and products of today make the jobs almost easy. Years ago I would slave for many hours fixing a section of broken cast iron drain line. Today you simply replace it with plastic than can be cut with a hand saw and glued together.

I say all that to say that times are vastly different. Despite the fact that we have a lot of time saving devices, we have less time. We have found more things to occupy ourselves so that it seems we are always busy. Cell phones ring everywhere. They are not even cell phones anymore, but are hand-held computers that can receive calls. We need to be occupied throughout the day. No time to waste on thought or contemplation we must keep moving. Back in my childhood the children had to pitch in and help with things. No more. Children are occupied just like we are during every waking moment. They carry video games, watch movies in cars, text message their friends, stare into the computer that is theirs, because everyone must have their own, and basically avoid conversation with their parents, just as their parents avoid conversation with them and each other.

Years ago people, who may have averaged a tenth grade education, read the newspaper, conversed with neighbors, went to community meetings, parent-teacher conferences, high school sporting events and took part in each others lives. Most could answer a question about current events or geography. Today, many of us don't know the name of the vice president. What does it have to do with marriage? Everything.

We have become narcissistic. Life is about us and the people around us are the supporting cast in the story of our lives. We cannot understand it when people disagree with us. Those who disagree have a character flaw. Into this uncertain personal development comes the question of marriage and what role it should play in life in community and in our country.

As a country we need stable family development. Families are at the root of a successful country. A family is the microcosm of the world. Who could be more different than a man and a woman, and yet under the right circumstances they become like one. There are geese that unite for life. They come together raise goslings and live happily ever after. They are devoted to each other and develop skills in protecting their young. When one goose is away gathering food or accomplishing some task, the other assumes full responsibility for the care of the young. They share tasks and seem happy to do it. How did they learn to do what they do? Some might call it patterning. This was a term used in psychology to describe the inexplicable. For example a young bird is found still in the egg and raised away from other birds of like type. These birds fly to Florida for the winter. When the laboratory raised bird is freed upon reaching adulthood, the other birds like him/her have already left for Florida. The released bird begins the flight alone and finds the other birds upon arrival in sunny Florida. Do we likewise have some pattern that instinctively tells us to mate and raise little humans. If we do television and fast food have obliterated the patterns.

We need to return to a strong family unit. The benefits should be obvious but bear repeating. Children raised by a mother and father are happier and more successful. Children raised by a mother and father who are happy with each other also fair better than those who are not. A survey of people in prison, on welfare, and others who have opted out of productive society are much more likely to have come from a single parent or no parent home. Grandparents aside, there is a negative aspect to life for a youngster whose parents do not care enough about him/her to be around to help the child grow and mature. That alone is enough for us to want to address the situation, however, it is much worse. Those children who have been in unhappy environments all of their lives tend to have children for whom they do not care. Relations with people of the opposite sex have no meaning except for sex. These people and their children make up a large portion of those who occupy the roles of the welfare system and they are also found in families with varying degrees of wealth. For those who are supported by the Welfare system, the childbirth and childcare are all taking place at a direct cost to the taxpaying public. When they are in touch with the criminal justice system, it is at the taxpayers expense. The government never tells us the total cost of the programs that care for the broken family people, because they don't want us to know. The government's elected officials use the programs as a tool of re-election by promising the people who are recipients things that the rest of the taxpayers will have to pay for, but never know the cost.

Just think, when an errant youth gets in trouble with the law, we provide the youth with a public defender. The pay of the defender is derived from tax dollars. The public defender, if the case is serious, will sometimes be replaced with a Court appointed lawyer with some criminal trial background. This is to insure that the indigent accused person gets a fair trial. That lawyer is paid with tax dollars. Both the public defender and/or the Court appointed lawyer will use investigators to seek out witnesses and background information to insure that the defense is as prepared as the prosecution. The investigators are paid with tax dollars. On the other side the police and the prosecutor are working to insure that the case is well prepared for Court. Witnesses are found and interviewed. Criminal abstracts are obtained on all witnesses and participants in the trial so that no surprises derail the prosecution. The prosecutors, the police and all of the witness fees, if necessary, are paid from taxpayers dollars. When the case goes to Court, everyone in the room who works for the Court system is being paid by the taxpayer. The Judge, the court clerk, stenographer, crier, security etc. are all on the taxpayers' payment list. If the errant youth is held in prison or detention until the trial he or she will be staying in a public facility, fed and clothed on the taxpayers money, guarded and transported on the taxpayers money and guarded at the time of trial by a sheriff or guard who is on the payroll.

And then, just think if the case is a capital murder case. There is a sentencing hearing and if the death penalty is imposed, the appeals begin and last for years. All or almost all of the lawyers involved in appeals are being paid by the taxpayers. Again there are investigators, judges and stenographers who must record every word.

Just think if that person had come from a happy home with a loving mother and father. How many millions would the taxpayers have saved? There would also be a non-victim who would not have been robbed, raped or killed.

The taxpayers not only pay for the criminal justice system's cost when a family breaks, the taxpayer may pay damages to the victim. If a party is injured in the course of being the victim of criminal behavior, it is likely that the taxpayer will be paying the hospital bill and any losses caused by the injuries suffered by the victim.

In addition to the all of the foregoing, if the criminal has a family of his or her own, being caught up in the criminal justice system may take away the earning capacity of the criminal and his or her family may fall into poverty and qualify benefits at the taxpayer's expense.

Having said all of that, it is the tip of the iceberg. Bad families cost us all in money and emotional strain more than we could calculate. Therefore, it is not only in our interest, but it is our duty to try to remedy this ugly situation. We recognize the problem because there have been many sociological studies that point out the decline of the family and the divorce rate, and the crime rate and the fact that the worst criminals generally come from broken homes, and on and on.

However, for the most part all that we do is wring our hands and somehow hope that by pointing out the statistics everyone will say, "lets make it better."

My suggestion is to start around the sixth grade when a child is eleven years old or twelve and begin the process of teaching about family life. Household budgets, parenting responsibilities, homemaking skills, the method of choosing a profession and pursuing a profession, how to write a resume, how to instill discipline into the life of your child, the definition of love and the definition of lust, and much more. Education must prepare children for life not just employment.

I know doctors and lawyers, police and firefighters who are good at their jobs and lousy at their marriage and childrearing skills. There is no excuse not to try to elevate the quality of life by training youngsters how to make the most important decisions of their lives. The doctors and lawyers, police and firefighters that I know who are lousy at marriage and childrearing are unhappy, miserable people who oftentimes escape their shortcomings at work. They avoid the dilemma of real life with their employment life. While they are providing positively to the community through work, they drag the community down by adding more undisciplined youngsters and young adults to the population. These professionally secure people may even, at times, add to the misery of life by their own actions or inactions. The problems of today, existed in the 1950s, however, statistically, it was for all intents and purposes non-existent. I was there.

MEDICINE AND THE LAW

Most of us today are concerned about health insurance. Politicians argue that we need a government sponsored health insurance plan that would cover everyone. It is reported that a great number of people have no health coverage at all. Some of those that are insured are covered by an employee health system that is received in a wage package. I have no basis for the following, except for the people that I know and meet as a result of my employment and social life, but I'll say it regardless. I think that people who need medical care get it. People who are uninsured get help from charity or just don't pay the medical bills, but they get it. We have the most advanced medical system in the world. People come here for treatment from everywhere in the world. The only time I heard of people leaving this country for treatment, was when they thought that some unproven treatment regimen that was not recognized here might help their incurable situation.

The government has squandered our Social Security money. The government cost of building far exceeds the cost to private enterprise. They have totally screwed up the finance system by their infernal tweaking of the mortgage approval requirements in an attempt to influence a voting bloc. We are in economic trouble with deficit spending that one day will cause us a great deal of trouble. The system of permits and inspections in local communities is a scam to bring income into the local government and exercise control over people who need not be controlled. What makes anyone think that the government would be able to manage the healthcare system. The reality is that the only reason they mention it is to get votes from people who do not think things through. Just imagine if you needed healthcare and had to report to Motor Vehicle for clearance to see a doctor.

Sometime in the early to middle sixties a University undertook a study of the Philadelphia Police Department. The study looked at the management of the department and the supervision of the many functions of a metropolitan police department. At the conclusion the study report stated that if the Philadelphia Police Department was building Chevrolets, they would cost $34,000.00. At the time Chevrolets cost about $4,000.00. Someone just said over the radio, that according to some think tank who studies such things, that today, July (sometime around the middle of the month) 2008 was the day that you began to work for yourself. If you were employed your tax burden collectively was more than half of your yearly pay. If the government takes over our healthcare, it may be November or December before we finish our obligation to the government and specialist referrals will require a trip to the Motor Vehicle Department.

Some people say that the problem with the healthcare system is lawyers. They posit that lawyers sue doctors and hospitals for malpractice and the insurance costs have risen so dramatically that it has made the cost of healthcare prohibitive. The problem with that conclusion is that juries award damages to lawyer's clients when they find that a doctor or hospital or pharmaceutical company has erred and caused injury. Some of the injuries caused are very serious. Some of the injuries are not. Some client's are truly injured and some are merely seeking a payday.

To make a proper determination of the issue of malpractice we need to explore the total issue. First, assume that a doctor has made a mistake and misdiagnosed his/her patient. The true problem went undiscovered for a period of over six months and worsened considerably, while the misdiagnosis was being followed. The patient went to a second doctor who bad-mouthed the first doctor. (This type of behavior is widely recognized in both the legal and medical professions where it is felt that when someone else is knocked down I am elevated) The damages are set at this point. The condition may take longer to bring under control or worse, it may be irreversible. The six months of suffering is a damage. The additional treatment period is a damage. The effect on loved ones is a damage. The effect on one's employment is a damage.

Enter the lawyer. The patient/client sees a lawyer and explains the error. The lawyer must determine the failure to diagnose as the proximate cause of the injury and that the failure to diagnose was in fact negligence. In order to do that the lawyer must find a doctor of equal stature with the offending doctor who will testify that the failure to diagnose was negligent. Usually, the doctor who bad-mouthed the other doctor and planted the seed of litigation will not testify against a colleague from the same medical community. A doctor from outside of the radius of the local community must be hired as an expert. The cost of the expert can be in the tens of thousands of dollars.

Depositions are taken by the patient/client's lawyer and they cost thousands. The doctor's insurance company has to hire a law firm to represent the doctor and they take depositions as well, that cost thousands. Experts must be hired to testify regarding the losses of the client. These experts discuss the loss of quality of life, the inability to do normal functions that others do regularly, the inability to work and create income and more. These experts are important to run up the jury's opinion of the losses suffered by the patient/client. Their testimony is a must and comes at a high price. It is not uncommon for the file to require expenditures of $40,000 to $50,000 at the lower end and into the hundreds of thousands at the high end to bring the matter to trial. Obviously the lawyers fees and the expenses come off the top. Sounds great for the lawyer but he or she must still win.

On the other side, the insurance company cannot settle a case without the doctor's permission. Doctors and lawyer are two of only a handful of people who can dictate that to the insurance company. A doctor's reputation and standing in the medical community is at stake. Insurance companies spend a great deal of money defending these cases. The win rate for the doctors and the insurance companies are high, but when they lose its news and the price tag can be huge.

Does it have to be that way. Of course not. There are a multitude of ways to handle "malpractice." First we should recognize that no one is perfect. We all make mistakes. To think that a doctor or a lawyer should be different from the rest of us is ridiculous. When I have accident clients in my office I love to describe damages of negligent behavior. In the first scenario you are rushing down the street and turn the corner in the blind and no one is there and you rush on. In the second scenario you are rushing down the street and turn the corner in the blind and a young boy is walking the other way and you clumsily bump into him and knock him to the ground. You are apologetic and help him up. He has an abrasion on his knee so you walk him home. His mother says thanks for bringing him home and says that she'll wash it up and put some mercurochrome on it and a band-aid. You give the boy some money and leave. In the third scenario you are rushing down the street and turn the corner in the blind and run into an 80 year old man. When you clumsily knock him to the ground he falls into the curb and breaks his hip. An ambulance takes the man to the hospital and he is admitted, develops pneumonia and dies. Three identical acts of negligence and three totally different results. The measure of damages is related to the victim. How many times have we done something negligent and no one is hurt and we think no harm no foul. The red light we failed to stop for, bumping into someone when we move without caution, the possibilities are endless. To act as though we cannot make a mistake is absurd.

There are so many things that can happen in the medical field which can create damages. In the first place most people in the care of a physician, regardless of their age are scenario threes. They are already sick and weakened or they wouldn't be there. Doctors, nurses, technicians can make mistakes just as anyone else in the world and this fact must be recognized if a solution to this problem affecting our medical care is to be solved. The mistake of someone in the medical field can have catastrophic results or go unnoticed. We have all heard the story about the person whose leg was to be amputated and the doctor operated on the wrong leg. I recently heard that one hospital had the patient write something on the leg which was not subject of surgery to overcome this type of mistake. (Maybe like, "No the other leg stupid") That information on the radio could have been a fake, but I doubt it. Doctors perform numerous medical procedures on any number of people in the same day, it is not hard to put ourselves in their place and see how a mistake could be made. We call overly careful people anal, but when seeking medical treatment we should start by asking the person providing service, "Are you anal?" If they answer yes then we could rest easier.

Let's just agree that things happen. We should also agree that we are different than other people in some ways and in fact we are different today than we were yesterday. For example, I am getting older each day as is everyone else. In our youth we grow for a number of years. Then there is a period of growth stagnation during which any changes are miniscule. Then as we pass middle age (whenever that might be) we begin to lose height. Just as we change in height and other outward physical respects we change inside. I used to enjoy riding on amusements such as the roller coaster and other rough rides. No more. Now those rides make me feel sick. My point here is that medicines that work for you today might make you sick tomorrow. Furthermore, medicines that work for thousands of other people might make you sick. There are people who feel a sense of loss when a medication is removed from the marketplace because it had worked for them. The removal could have been related to someone having a bad reaction to the medication, but the person who would miss the drug had been successfully taking it for a long period and been provided relief.

How do we fix this problem? Well, we should start by agreeing that it is a problem. When some innocent person is injured as result of taking a medication properly for a condition that the medication is produced to remedy, they deserve to be made whole. The medical community and the pharmaceutical community must agree that accidents happen and innocent people get hurt. Anyone who claims to have been injured would first make a report to the medical police. (I use the word police because I like the word, but I really mean a medical investigator) People with a medical background should staff the medical police department either fulltime or part-time. Their pay would come from the medical profession by having a percentage of medical bills include a surcharge for the police. Ideally, the police staff could be retired or retiring medical people, such as surgeons who can no longer, or should no longer perform surgeries. The medical police would have subpeona powers and be able to bypass HIPPA regulations and such so they could truly and thoroughly investigate all complaints.

The police would also have the power to interview anyone who would have any relationship to the complaint, including doctors, nurses and others. They would have the power to order a person to submit to a lie detector examination and if they refused would be able to infer from the refusal a level of deception. They would be able to report the offending person to their employer as uncooperative.

At the conclusion of the investigation by the medical police department, if they found fault they would determine whether there was a willingness on the errant medical provider to remedy the situation. If the answer was affirmative, the matter could be referred to damage specialists. These people could come from the insurance community or be specially trained for this purpose. A damage amount could be determined and offered to the injured party. If accepted the insurance carried for this purpose would pay the claim. If the errant medical provider did not accept the findings of the medical police and the damage specialist, the injured party would be notified and advised that they could file suit against the provider. The injured party would be able to call the medical police specialist who chaired the investigation as a witness and within the confines of evidentiary law, the specialist could testify as to findings and conclusions. Polygraph results and confidential information should not be testified to without permission of the person from whom it was garnered. The errant medical provider and the insurance company could work out who would be responsible for the result of the lawsuit if it exceeded the recommended amount proposed by the damage specialist and agreed to by the injured party.

Any injured party would be compelled to submit their medical claim for evaluation prior to filing suit. This type of procedure would compel even the most reluctant medical provider to admit to a mistake. The benefit would be to streamline the matter and dispose of it without the enormous cost of trial. Insurance companies would benefit by more reasonable settlements and would create a climate with their insured either through cooperation or penalty to admit to the truth of the situation and work toward a solution. Often times a doctor is reluctant to admit an error. This reluctance could be based in ego or fear of a diminished reputation. Universal acknowledgement that things can go wrong even when people with expertise and extreme carefulness perform the most routine of matters would be a byproduct of this type solution. The acknowledgement would take some of the sting out being the subject of a medical investigation.

Another even more important benefit from an open dialogue between the all of the parties could lead to a better form of treatment, better care in administering drugs, better care in testing drugs prior to their admission to the general public and many other unstated benefits to all parties, medical providers and medical service recipients. If we all accept that mistakes can be made, we would all look to the process to find ways to remedy the mistakes. Like writing, "the other leg, stupid" on the leg we wanted to save.

Who would be hurt? Large law firms which specialize in medical malpractice and insurance companies. The law firm needs no explanation, but the insurance companies objection may. Premiums are based on need and risk. The primary driving force of the elevated premiums for medical providers is the risk that the insurance company undertakes when assuming the responsibility for covering errors of doctors and other providers. Lawmakers have recently expanded the time for someone to file a lawsuit from the normal statute of limitations of two years to the time when a child reaches maturity and then two years. This means that an insurance company could be on the hook for twenty years (plus) after the birth of a child. This required some severe re-evaluation of premiums and drove some OB-GYNs from the practice or to states that did not honor the statute of limitation modification.

Insurance premiums are an unknown quantity to most of us. Insurance companies use actuary tables to determine life expectancy when charging premiums. However, when, from the time you sign on the line and the time you reach the age you are supposed to expire, there is a chance that the actuary tables have been modified upward. (Ergo the sixties and seventies are the new middle age) The insurance companies have been collecting premiums on the old data for years. Likewise, when they project the amount of money that they need to cover the potential lawsuits twenty years in the future they are using actuary tables based upon outdated information. Medical procedures are modifying almost exponentially today. Knee replacements and hip replacement for example have become more patient friendly in the last ten years. The recovery period is much shorter and much less painful. The results from the procedure are also much better. The same thing is true in almost every facet of the medical profession. The risk of error is much less today than ten years ago and ten years from now exponentially much less. But the premiums keep rolling in.

The law profession has been briefly touched on but also needs to be explored. Having been involved in the law as a police officer and lawyer for close to fifty years, I have not seen everything, but I feel that I have seen enough to comment.

The first matter would be the manner in which we appoint judges. In the two states that I am licensed, judges are appointed in one and elected in the other. Your first thought would be that the state in which judges were elected would be fairer and the judges of better quality. Not necessarily. As we discussed earlier, we don't know much about the person we turn the keys to the country over to, so how much study are we going to give to the person on the ballot to become a judge. The Governor who appoints judges would be a little better able to select people of quality because the appointees would reflect directly upon the Governor. However, the people under review by the political party in one state and the Governor in the other are recommended by political people and sometimes the first qualification is the amount of support the proposed candidate has given the respective party.

Having said that, most of the judges that I have encountered over the years are endeavoring to do a good job. There are some that are not. The problem is the power that they hold. In family court, they control the lives of mothers, fathers and children and can dramatically alter the course of someone's life. In civil court they can rule against you for sums of money which could ruin your finances for life. In criminal court they can and have convicted innocent people and sentenced them to prison. Some might argue that the system requires (if the parties elect) that a jury can decide the fate of a civil case or criminal case. While this is true, the judge controls the amount and type of information that the jury hears and by the judge's actions the jury can sometimes determine which way the judge would rule and lean that way. Juries themselves can be unfair. The members could be prejudice, not only to race or nationality, but to people who are attractive or unattractive. It is certainly easier to believe an attractive person unless you are unattractive and feel threatened by the person testifying. In short, we trust our fate to a person who has never met either party prior to the testimony, but at the conclusion of the testimony must make a decision that one is to believed and the other not be believed. For the serious jurist the weight must be very heavy to bear, for the not serious jurist, not so much.

Judges suffer from the same malady that celebrities, news media people, supervisors, executives and many more suffer from, power. The power makes everything they say or think right. The people around them who are beholden to them would never criticize or second guess. They would be supportive and ego builders. Judges, therefore, think that they are right. I have heard many lecture someone that they have found at fault or otherwise ruled against. They lectured them concerning their behavior. The thought that they could be wrong doesn't enter their mind. In one respect they must develop that shield or they wouldn't be able to function. In some however, they relish the power of the position. In our country today the most powerful person seems to be the Supreme Court Judge with the vote to make a majority opinion. I hope that Washington, Jefferson, Adams, Franklin, Patrick Henry and many more are not suffering through having to watch the country and government that they risked their lives for turn its back on the guiding principles that led us through the years and the many pitfalls along the way, to reach the success and place in the World that we enjoy today. I am afraid though, that like the Roman Empire, we will fail as a result of our own doing.

We need to rethink our approach to the system. For example, the one qualification to become a judge is to be a lawyer. However, nothing in the educational requirements to become a lawyer has anything to do with determining whether someone is telling the truth or lying. Mock trial practice may seem to be a training course for finding the truth, but it is in fact a determination of preparation of witnesses. Forensic evidence is helpful in determining the truth during a trial, but when the decision to be made is between people testifying differently to a matter and only one can be telling the truth, there is no training in the law. Psychology on the other hand deals with determining the truth.

Science has a checkered past concerning criminality and the truth. A scientist developed a theory, that at the time was somewhat accepted, that, you could tell if someone was a criminal by the bumps on his head. Someone with a heavy brow was seen to be a person who could not be trusted. Neither was ever accepted as the best method. Two things that seem to hold some degree of promise today are the polygraph and pupil metrics. Neither is admissible in court, but either one would seem more promising than to rely on than the whim of a judge or a jury on a particular day.

Today's science would also be a welcome sentencing tool. Lawyers cannot pick the judge that will try the criminal case in which they represent a client. If they could the more lenient sentencing judge would be so busy that it could take years to bring a case to trial. Conversely, some of the strictest judges would have cobwebs on the doors to their courtrooms. If the prosecutors could do the selecting the roles would be reversed. In an anonymous questionnaire directed to lawyers, I believe that amongst criminal lawyers, very few would disagree with foregoing, but if their name was required, all would disagree. This fact should be disturbing to everyone. Why should the roulette wheel of justice (scheduling cases) be the determiner of severity or leniency for a particular defendant?

A thorough questionnaire at the end of a trial based upon the facts surrounding the crime and the facts about the defendant should be fed into a computer and the sentence, time in jail, determined by those factors. For example, if a working, loaded gun was used in the commission of a crime the sentence should be modified from someone who faked having a weapon, or brandished a weapon that was either fake or unloaded. To some extent the fear of the person having the crime committed against them would be the same but the danger would certainly be different. The computer could sentence someone to three years, four months, seven days, twelve hours and forty minutes, but who cares, it would be fairer.

At the end of some trials the defendant is convicted and sentenced, and still maintains his/her innocence. We hear of cases where someone has been in jail for years for a crime they did not commit. And in a few matters, even after DNA evidence clears them they have difficulty getting out of prison. Our system should accept the science of today and continue to investigate even after a person is sentenced. For example, the person who maintains their innocence and is willing to undergo a polygraph and if successful, sodium pentathol (truth serum), should have the right to demand further investigation. Having been both a police officer and a lawyer, I am sure of two things. One, there are many guilty people walking the streets after being found not guilty, or had their cases dismissed for any of a variety of reasons. Secondly, there are innocent people in jail. They may not be totally innocent, but they didn't commit the crime they are convicted of having committed. We cannot glibly think that well at least they got some time even if it's not for the crime they got away with. The error of this thinking is that someone not only did not get caught for the crime, but the crime is now thought of as solved, and no one is ever going to look again for the person who committed it.

Like much else in our society today, the administration of law enforcement is totally void of common sense. For example, if you steal a newspaper it is called theft. Theft is a felony if the item being stolen is above a certain amount of money, usually around two hundred dollars. Vandalism is a misdemeanor regardless of how much it costs to repair the vandalism. So figure this out. Someone steals your backyard grille. It could be one of those new domed things with side burners and all of the accessories and is valued at $1,500.00. It is a felony and the perpetrator could receive a serious jail sentence. On the other hand someone could take a can of spray paint and write obscenities all over your house. The cost of removing and repairing your home could be $3,000.00 and the crime is a misdemeanor with a not so serious sentence. Maybe the judge will sentence them to restitution and you can go to the trouble of trying to collect the funds from them. Both matters could be insured and cost you nothing or one could cost a great deal more than the other. In federal criminal matters, the severity of the sentence is guided by the amount of money involved. Why can't the same principle be used in matters of losses to an individual? In the crime of theft, one of the factors necessary to prove theft is that the perpetrator has the intent to permanently deprive the rightful owner of the property. This is why there is a crime called joyriding, which means that the taking of an automobile is not meant to permanently deprive its owner. If you have to pay to repair the vandalism you are permanently deprived of your money. If someone litters the front of your home and you must go outside with a broom and dustpan you are permanently deprived of the time it takes to pick up after someone else. People today say "That's five minutes I'll never get back," meaning that it was totally wasted time. Time is important. We have often heard that time is money. We get paid for spending time at work. Why is the time that we have to spend cleaning up after someone, who with callous disregard for anyone else litters the highway or the front of someone's home not so valuable.

We need to take these matters more seriously. Society has failed in the area of discipline. Parents, schools, and other adults have all failed in the quality of life arena. We should all be concerned about the things that affect our quality of life. Someone playing their radio loudly is rude and the person doing it means to be rude. This is a person who wants to be noticed and the only way to be noticed is to be rude. Children on public transportation are rude. They curse and talk very loudly. They play their music so loud that conversation with another rider is impossible. Teenagers walk around with their underwear showing so that you must notice them. This is really a form of celebrity for the malcontent.

We all need to know the rules of civility. The freedom you enjoy should not infringe on someone's enjoyment of life. Mayor Guiliani of New York has been held in high esteem by many for doing what most of wish we had the power to do. He ordered the police officers of New York City to enforce quality of life crimes. The result was that all crime went down. The relationship is unmistakable and yet there has been no rush for other communities to follow. Why do other communities not follow? My guess is that they want to have their own plan so they get credit. The important thing in political life is to take credit and attach blame. Actually solving a problem is not nearly as important as getting good press. Mayor Guiliani made a right choice, but the police officers did the work. The society of New York City as a whole accepted the effort and supported it, and if truth be told, were relieved when some bum didn't come up and spit on their window when they stopped for a traffic light. Mayor Guiliani did a great deal more than tell police officers to enforce quality of life crimes. Some of the other things he did should have caused him praise and some not so much. In political life though, to follow someone's proven method could cause one to be seen as heaping praise on that person and therefore, it is unacceptable, especially if it is someone from the other party.

The problem is just not with the political system. The lack of seeking solutions has befallen society as a whole. We have become the automatons of the future. We walk from place to place and follow instructions. We go home at night and the television tells us what we think in 15 second increments. For example, while I am writing this we are in the midst of prices going through the roof on gasoline. The question of drilling off shore or in Alaska is prominent. A news reporter reported that Congress is recessing without voting on lifting the ban against off shore drilling. The reporter went on to say that it would seem that there is sufficient support to lift the ban, but it would not make much difference because it will take ten years to see any oil coming from the off shore sites. He did not credit anyone with the statement regarding ten years, so it must either be his opinion or a well known fact. But is it? Why ten years? What investigation has the reporter conducted to determine that it would be ten years, and if so, what would take so long? The oil companies seem to know that the oil is there. There are oil drilling sites in the North Sea, in the Gulf of Mexico and other places, did they all take ten years? If the Oil companies are willing to spend the necessary funds to support a project that would not yield a profit for ten years, why are we so angry at them for the profits they make now? Perhaps the delay is because of obtaining the necessary government clearance and listening to all the whining by opponents who have no alternative solution, takes time.

Prior to making that statement the reporter should ask the oil companies the question in the following way; "If you could start tomorrow, exploring and building your platform and so forth, how long would it be before oil was brought to the surface? Maybe the reporter would learn that nine and a half years of the ten years is government interference.

All that aside, tomorrow I will hear people state with authority "what's the difference, we won't get any oil out of there for ten years." We all accept the reporter's comments.

We need to change. Not everyone is aggressive enough, but if someone were to say to a teenager on the elevated train, "pull up your pants and turn down the radio," at least we should stand up and applaud. If it caught on, it could turn us all around. We could become emboldened enough to say to our representatives, "What happened to the three hundred billion dollars the GAO says was wasted last year, through theft, incompetence and greed?" We could call the news station and ask, "By what authority does the reporter state that it will take ten years for off shore drilling to yield oil?" We could attend meetings if they hold them, of our local government authorities and find out why they spend so much of our money.

Another unquestionable fact is that if taxes are lowered, the economy grows and income to the government increases. Why then would anyone support a new tax? Politicians are all down on the oil companies for making a profit and tout as a solution taxing windfall profits. It sounds good, but there are questions that must be asked. For example: What is the profit margin? In other words what is the percentage of return on the dollars invested? Who is getting the profits? The answer to that question is easy, it is the stockholders. But if we tax the oil companies profits, how about taxing other companies who make excessive profits? How do we determine which profits are excessive? The common knowledge is that Supermarkets have a small margin of profit, perhaps ten percent. Furniture stores and jewelry shops have a much larger profit margin. So the grocery store only makes ten cents on a one dollar item, and the jeweler makes one hundred dollars on a two hundred dollar item. The grocer would still make a lot of money because of the quantity, and the jeweler could have a hard time paying his bills because of the lack of quantity. Another issue with all businesses is investment versus income. The outrage against the oil companies came as result of the company stating its quarterly profit.

The profit was in the billions and was higher than any previous profit. The important question is, "How much did the profit mean to each stockholder and what was the relationship between their investment (the original cost of the stock) and the return?"

That is important because we need only look to Bill Gates to see someone who made a huge profit from his work and his investment. Are we going to take his money away? How about the other computer things, like Amazon.com and many more? What was their profit-to-investment margin? Are we going to allow the government to take away their profit margins? Xerox, Polariod, Viagra, the list is endless for successful products that have made huge profits. Only a fool would want the government to have access to taxing windfall profits. The incentive to invent and produce would be gone. More importantly, the government would not thrive because of the income. The income to the government has increased and increased and we are still in debt. In fact, the more money the government takes in the more debt we have.

Back to the law. But first another reference to common sense. I do not have enough information at hand to make a determination about the war in Iraq. At first I thought it made no sense. Iraq was no threat to us, thought I, why bother? Later, I thought, if we need to flex our muscles in the Middle East, it might as well be in Iraq. (This is based upon the belief that many of those in power in the Middle East hate us and wish we were dead. If left unchecked they could be a true threat to our country) All things considered if my logic is correct, we didn't do so bad. Most people think the war is a failure, but I do not. We have lost over four thousand valiant Americans in Iraq. There are many more who have been injured. That is awful. However, statistically a good number of the Americans in Iraq would have been killed here had they not been in Iraq. Think of the numbers of Americans murdered and maimed every year in crimes. Think of the number of Americans killed every year by drunk drivers. Think of the numbers of Americans killed in auto accidents. Why don't we exhibit the same displeasure over those deaths of Americans? I recently heard a statistic that I am not sure is true, but I'll repeat it anyhow. "Over twelve thousand people will be killed this year by either accidents or crimes that involve an illegal alien." What's up with that?

We spend a fortune on our government which includes all facets of the law and law enforcement. We are the customers. If we didn't like the service in a restaurant we wouldn't go there. If others felt the same, the restaurant would soon go out of business. We are forced to be the customers of a business that cannot be forced out of business no matter how badly the business operates and no matter how badly the business treats us. The government doesn't treat us like customers. We need to demand the service we are entitled to receive.

No matter who gets the credit or the blame we need to enforce quality of life crimes. We enforce cockamamie political correctness laws. Go back a couple pages to the vandalism example. If the person who spray painted our house put a racial slur, a religious reference or an ethnic comment, vandalism wouldn't be simply vandalism, it would be a hate crime. That would make it much more serious. How come? The damage and the cost of repair should make it serious enough. Besides, it's the paint and the visualization of destruction that show the real lack of feeling for civilized life. Is the fact that the vandal doesn't make it personal in words make it any less personal when your residence is being disrespected and damaged? It wouldn't be very comforting to say to yourself, well the vandal caused $4,000.00 worth of damage to my home and inconvenienced me greatly while the necessary repairs are being made, but at least the vandal doesn't hate me because I'm (Black, Jewish, Catholic, White, Muslim, or some other category of people who can be insulted by another).

What is lacking is common sense. There must be give and take in the creation of laws and the arm of enforcement. What are we trying to accomplish by passing laws. In Philadelphia in the 1960s there was a horrible rape of a mother and daughter. The legislature rushed to pass a law to increase the penalty for rape. The law did not apply to the person who committed the rape because you cannot make an ex post facto law. (A law that applies to acts already committed) The legislature was responding to public sentiment and trying to make points with the voters rather than do their job for the entire population of the State. This example is just one of many. Most of the legislation created has very little effect on the population other than to affect our purse strings. What this has created is a population looking to get something back from government. School loans, help with the mortgage, welfare, subsidies, economic stimulus etc. are the bones with no meat that are thrown out to the population and used create a good thought for the legislature that is handing out the largesse. What is the common sense against it? IT WAS OUR MONEY TO START WITH. When they take it and then give it back it costs us more than we benefit. First we have to pay them collect our money. Think of the agencies involved in collecting our money. We pay them all. Then think of the agencies necessary to get some of it back. They have to draft checks and mail them to all of us. We have to pay them all and the postage too. (Even when there is no postage on the envelope we are paying the delivery charge)

Give a thought to capital gains. When you buy a home you pay the market price. When you sell a home you get the market price. Where is the capital gain? Your mom and dad (or grand-mom and grand-pop) bought a home in the 1940s for $4,000.00. The same house is worth $150,000.00 today. In the 1940s your dad probably made less than a dollar an hour and now you might make forty dollars an hour. If you had the same job as your dad or grand-pop you would be making forty times a much and a comparable house would cost forty times as much. Where is the gain in capital? You could also come to the same conclusion is you looked to the rate of inflation or the value of a dollar.

The government now wants to be involved in our healthcare. You might ponder why? There used to be a senator who was a doctor, Are they going to ask him to run the system? There might be a person or two who had some experience in the insurance world. Are they going to run the billing and payment element of healthcare? No. What is happening here is the legislature is going to get votes from people by showing they care about the plight of all of the citizens by taking care of all of their medical needs. Then they are going to create another government bureaucracy that, once created, will take on as a first responsibility its own longevity. Healthcare will be a system of red tape and approvals for any service rendered. Going postal will be replaced by going medical. After a few years of reporting to the Motor Vehicle Bureau for medical treatment, we will become as Canada and

Europe have become. If you can afford medical treatment you will go to another country where doctors have the freedom to treat patients without governmental interference. Perhaps you would go to one of the Caribbean Islands.

Has government run amok? Yes, but at our insistence. We want the government to solve all of our problems and listen to all of our complaints. This country was formed by people who were getting away from repressive governments. Originally it was religious freedom, but lately it has been political freedom. Our current economy is in the tank, but it will recover and our economy is why many of our recent emigrates have sought to come to our shores. Having said that, it is not enough to rest on our laurels and say "Well at least we are better than country X, otherwise people would not leave there to come here." We should be continuing in the spirit of those who risked life and limb hundreds of years ago to start this wonderful country. They wanted government to bring civilization and order. They wanted to be left alone. They wanted to work at their trade, raise their families, and flourish from their own efforts. Now it seems we want cradle to grave care. If we don't make enough to take care of ourselves, we want the government to take the money from someone who earns more and use it to take care of us. We have bought into the statement of the government's elected officials, who take credit for everything positive and never raise issues of negativity. For example, one of our elected officials indicated that we would have a cure for cancer before the turn of the century. (The turn of the century occurred over eight years ago and while inroads have been made in the medical profession for the treatment of cancer, it hasn't been cured.) No one raises the statement as a question to the politician. But the reality is the same as the reality for going to the moon. The president can say it, but it is the American spirit and ingenuity as well as the capitalist underpinnings of our system that bring about change. I know of no case of a politician applying for a patent for some scientific discovery or medical cure.

Automobiles, Energy & The Environment

We have recently gone through a spike in the price of crude oil. Gasoline at the pump went to over four dollars in some locations. At this writing the price has dropped by about seventy-five cents. The drop appears to have been brought about by reduced demand. In other words, the oil market found the price where consumers would take it upon themselves to reduce usage which makes the suppliers realize that there is maximum we will pay and then we won't buy as much. Reduced demand of any product in any marketplace is a bad thing for the suppliers. Too much demand is a bad thing for consumers. Too much demand in the oil marketplace is the worst.

Oil affects all sources of transportation, rail, truck, bus, airlines and personal cars. All of the products that we consume are brought to us by the use of oil. Whenever we travel farther than we can walk, we use oil. Even electric vehicles use oil. Many of the products that we use every day are made with oil. Plastics, carpet, synthetic materials all are produced using oil. Styrofoam cups and foam rubber are made by using oil.

Therefore, when oil goes up so does almost everything else. When the American consumer cuts down on the mileage of his or her personal car, they aren't shopping, traveling and using the products of oil, nor are they buying the products of oil. The oil suppliers (whoever they are) made a tactical error. They thought that the Americans would accept the price that Europeans have been paying for years. We didn't. The suppliers made a tidy profit in the short term, and will probably recover quickly over the long term. But, they may have unleashed the

American spirit which during Second World War had us producing war materials at a phenomenal rate.

The government has jumped into the fray trying to position themselves as the solver of all problems and the provider of all answers. Once again, they have missed the boat. The government's role has and should always be that of a policeman. We need the protection of the government from foreign enemies who would take over our country. We need the protection of the government from law breakers who would harm us or steal from us. We also need the protection of the government to protect us from unscrupulous business people who would sell us dangerous products or who would harm our environment. Over the last fifty years, many of the rivers in our country have become much cleaner as a result of the government policing the people who used our waterways as their own private dump. During the same period the air we breathe has become much cleaner due to a reduction in the emissions from factories and automobiles. While the government has played a role, don't give them all the credit. The automobile manufacturers have played a huge role in the betterment of the air we breathe.

My first car was a 1949 Plymouth. I was the only one in the family with a driver's license, so at sixteen, (in 1955) my parents bought me a car. The responsibilities that came with the car were that I had to chauffer my mom and dad to work and back and occasionally had to transport my older sister. The car had a heater, but no radio. It was a stick shift six cylinder. The car got about eighteen to twenty miles to the gallon. Gasoline during the years when I first began to drive was sometimes less than twenty cents a gallon, but for the most part probably a quarter a gallon. The Plymouth ran good and its life expectancy was about 75,000 to 90,000 miles. We had purchased it used, and it had probably about 20,000 miles when we got it. My last three cars were purchased new and each was sold running very well with 150,000 miles on the odometer. My Plymouth let out a puff of smoke when I accelerated; my last three cars appeared to have nothing coming from the tailpipe. The Plymouth was fussy when it was cold or raining causing me great trepidation when I tried to start the car. The only time the last three refused to start quickly was upon the demise of the battery.

What's the difference? Fuel injection and the use of onboard computers. Between the Plymouth and the last three vehicles, I had a 1969 Bonneville convertible, a 1973 Cadillac Coupe, a 1969 Cadillac Sedan Deville, a Dodge muscle car and a bunch of others. The four I named ran on high test and got between five miles and ten miles to the gallon. The last three vehicles I owned ran on regular, had more luxury and equipment than the previous cars, and all got just shy of twenty miles per gallon in local traffic driving. On the road they all ran sparingly close to twenty-five miles per gallon.

I have had some limited personal experience with automobiles and some professional. I represent, as an attorney, people in the auto business, from repair shops to car dealers and from recycle yards to engine re-builders. The conclusion that I draw from that experience is that automobile engines run better and longer because the gasoline is consistently mixed at the proper proportion with air and that the explosion in the cylinder is precisely timed to convert all of the gasoline into force. In addition, much work has been performed to synchronize the transmission to the engine to gain the best use of the force produced. This increase in performance is accompanied by equipment that wasn't even dreamed of in the 1949 Plymouth. Most of the equipment that we take for granted runs off of the energy produced by the engine and the electric generated by the engine force. Needless to say, if the car was stripped like my Plymouth, the mileage would increase.

What President, Vice President, Senator, Congressman, Mayor, Alderman or Councilperson had anything to do with the innovations found in our automobiles? My guess is none. Did any of them have something to do with the impetus behind the innovations? Absolutely. We were aware of the poison that was being spewed out the tailpipes of the American (for that matter all) cars, buses and trucks. Politicians responded to our worries. Studies by medical professionals and other scientists produced irrefutable evidence that the emissions were harmful. Capitalism jumped to the bait, because there was money to be made. New fuel systems, new transmissions, and the fine accessories that we all enjoy were the result. There are people throughout the auto industry getting royalties on their inventions that have yielded the superior vehicles we now drive.

Now to today. We have barred oil companies from drilling because it will harm our environment. What about the drilling going on elsewhere in the World? Won't that harm our environment? People responsible for oil spills in this country are subject to civil prosecution. Why would anyone take the chance of not using the best technology available? I am a proud American, and I am sure that we are better shepherds of the environment in the United States than folks overseas. Why shouldn't we take the forefront in developing the best technology for extracting oil? Politicians argue that we need to develop alternative energy. I certainly agree. However, common sense tells me that we are far from divorcing ourselves from oil. We use oil in too many products and there are too many gasoline and diesel powered vehicles in use. If we developed a usable fuel cell vehicle tomorrow, would we order everyone to scrap their fossil fueled vehicle immediately? And would we demand that every homeowner and landlord immediately replace the heating system in their properties? Would we park the buses, trains and trucks until they were adapted to the fuel cell? Would the American public be forced to swallow the cost of the vehicle replacement? Not without a gun to our heads.

I have never seen a fuel celled vehicle. I have spoken to people who have an interest in the development, and I have been told that the power plant is totally different than the internal combustion engine in our cars. Therefore, it is safe to assume that we are not going to perform some simple modification to our vehicle and drive off with a tank full of water.

We still need oil and we should try to supply ourselves. We need the work. We need the money, and we need to stop giving away our trade balance. If we were sure that the money we sent overseas was going to be used to buy our tractors and surplus food products, there wouldn't be an issue. But, some of us feel, me included, that the money we send overseas is being used to harm us. At the very least, it is not being used to make people our friends.

When we are able to mass produce some type of alternate fuel vehicle, it will take years to wean us off of oil. In fact, considering the many uses of oil, we will never be in a place where we won't need some oil production. Current technology has never gotten us close to any type of alternative that would get us away from using oil where two metal surfaces rub together.

Alternative fuels are another answer. Biofuels and other alternate fuels are an option, but will take years to supply enough to replace the current demand for oil. Can we possibly grow enough food stocks to extract fuel and still have enough to eat? Probably in time. There are innumerable scientific projects currently studying ways to increase the production of food crops. There are also studies underway to grow algae. Oil has been extracted from algae and has been refined to a fuel replacement. In fact, recently, a passenger aircraft (empty, but for the crew) flew a few hundred miles using only an algae based fuel. There is promise in these alternate fuels because they do not alter dramatically the rolling stock traveling the highways of the United States. These fuels would be distributed in the same fashion and probably by the same companies that distribute gasoline and diesel. Furthermore the tax obligation on the driving public would be easily collected. That money which is supposed to be used for road repair would still be available to the coffers of the U.S. Treasury. How would the government get their money if all you needed to go coast to coast was water?

The situation with nuclear power is almost amusing, if it wasn't so serious. Again, as with most everything else written before, I present the disclaimer. I have no scientific knowledge of nuclear power. My information comes from the public record. My knowledge is that I am aware of nuclear power, of nuclear bombs, nuclear submarines and warships and other uses for nuclear energy. I call the microwave by the name given by others, the nuke. Having said that, I still have an opinion based on my common sense that nuclear power is a dangerous but controllable material.

Over the years we have developed expertise with nuclear power to create energy in dramatic fashion. A nuclear submarine can be propelled by a nuclear reactor for long periods of time without requiring fuel stops. When I was on a destroyer in 1958, we would take trips that required being met at sea by a tanker so that we could obtain sufficient fuel to complete our trip. For example, during the one summer, we took a midshipman's cruise. We went from Norfolk Virginia to Norway and then to Northern Spain and finally to Monaco. We were assigned about ten or twelve midshipmen from the Naval Academy and they learned about the ship by changing jobs every so often. Many times during the cruise we met with a Tanker and had to refuel. We also refueled in port. A nuclear submarine can travel for months and probably longer without needing to do anything to keep its power plant operating. The nuclear submarine "Skate" was commissioned during my time in the Navy and to the best of my knowledge there have been no accidents with nuclear power in ships or submarines. It has been almost forty-eight years since I was discharged from the Navy.

In the commercial use of nuclear power there were two famous accidents, "Three Mile Island" in Pennsylvania and "Chernobyl" in Russia. To the best of my recollection no one was injured in the Three Mile Island mishap, but people were affected by the nuclear leak in Chernobyl.

In speaking of automobiles I directed your attention to the marvelous revolution in automobiles in a most positive way. Today's automobiles have climate control, heated and cooled seats, seats that are contoured for comfort and back support, dashboards that look like the interior of a 747 airplane, with controls and computers that tell you everything. In comparison a 1949 Plymouth had a heater. Why would we not feel that the industrial and scientific skills of our population and the population of other countries who use nuclear power have not made dramatic increases in knowledge regarding nuclear power? And that they have used this knowledge to take dramatic steps in making the reactors and fuel rods much safer and easily handled and stored. Many of the detractors cite the fact that the spent rods have to be buried or stored in some fashion that will keep them from affecting the population, such as under a mountain or in an abandoned mine. While that doesn't make me very happy, I am certain that American ingenuity and profit motivation could come up with a use for the spent rods. They still contain enough power to be deadly to people, but so are many of the things that we use every day. I remember a dog that I had years ago had heartworms. It is a terrible thing that can take the life of a dog. The heartworm is supposed to be transported by mosquitoes.

When the infected mosquito bites a dog, the heartworm enters the dog's blood system. As the worms grow the blood flow to the heart is choked off. The treatment for my dog was arsenic. Yes, the same arsenic used by the old lady in arsenic and old lace. The dosage was controlled to simply kill the worms and not the dog. The treatment was successful. My dog lived to his full life expectancy. Arsenic is deadly and so are fuel rods, but perhaps there is a use for the rods. There must be something left in them despite the fact that we call them spent rods. They are still dangerous. Maybe what makes them dangerous is powerful enough to have a further use. Maybe not. But I'll bet if the question was posed to entrepreneurs someone would work very hard to find a use. We used to pay people to take away the used fry oil from the fast food joints. Now there is a process for turning the waste oil into bio-diesel. Now the fast food joints will be selling it. Perhaps one day we will sell the spent rods for their secondary purpose and not bury them at all.

Common sense would lead one to believe that nothing is stagnant. If you can think it someone can do it. Flash Gordon was a spaceman of the 1950s. At the same time Dick Tracy was a detective with a wristwatch from which he could call the police station and other police officers. Neither was realistic when they were appearing in the comic strips. But the technology portrayed is old stuff now. I was in business school in the 1960s and was told that I had to buy a calculator for class. The calculator was similar to what is currently available in the dollar store and it cost approximately sixty dollars. Likewise, in 1949, there was a television for sale with a large cabinet and a nine or ten inch screen which sold for four hundred ninety-nine dollars. There were three channels, they went off at about eleven PM and the picture was black and white and not too clear. We have come far in the span of my life. There have been inventions in other countries too, but we have in past seemed to lead the way. Capitalism, in my opinion, was the catalyst for advancement. Altruism may be part of the motivation, but the ability to turn a profit is a strong driving force.

The first chapter addressed greed and pointed out that greed is the yearning for wealth without thought. People just seem to have the desire to be rich. They don't care how they get it, they just want it. Turning a profit has little to do with greed. Turning a profit is a confidence boost. It is an ego pumper. It's like winning a gold medal in the Olympics. Altruism is close in everyway to turning a profit. For the mentally stable person, being able to help another human being, or better yet multiple human beings, is a blast. No one needs to thank you or kiss your ring. Just knowing that you are capable of helping someone is a kick. There are innumerable people who would invest their own money with absolutely no hope of recovering it if they were working on a project that would benefit mankind. My wife worked as an unpaid volunteer in an animal refuge because she loves animals and wanted to help. She did make a difference in many ways, but mostly she worked with the animals to make them more adoptable. When the animal control officer drops off a dog or a person surrenders a pet, the animal is terrified, lonely and abandoned. My wife nurtured the animals back to mental health. She never made money from her work, nor did she become famous or envied by others. She quietly did her best and her reward was personal and deep.

What I am alluding to here is that there are people in the United States who will work to solve a problem to benefit others. They will work to solve a problem to make some money. And some will do it for both reasons. The important thing as that when problems are identified there are a great number of capable and well meaning people who are willing to help uncover the solution. The government does not have to jump into the breech for every situation that arises for the purpose of gaining notoriety. The government doesn't have to throw money (our money) at every problem they can conceive in hopes that someone outside the government will come up with a solution and they can take credit. A friend of mine worked in security in a laboratory setting with chemists and doctors seeking to cure cancer. They laboratory was funded by the United States Government with our money. My friend once joked that if a cure for cancer was uncovered by one of the doctors, he or she would never make it out of the laboratory alive. The cure would stop the funding and their paychecks.

My point here is that a problem is a challenge to many individuals. For altruistic motives or capitalist motives people will rush to the problem to find a solution. The government should not stand in the way or worse act like there is no solution. Americans want to drive their cars and are the market for any product which will keep their cars running, provide better fuel economy, provide a cleaner atmosphere, cut out noise pollution and save the polar bears and the seals. I know that the air is cleaner in Philadelphia than it was in past years and there are more cars than there were in past years. I know the Delaware river is cleaner than it was in past years. I know that industry has diminished in the Northeast, but the cleaner river is because people became interested in the river and public opinion went towards limiting dumping pollutants. Gasoline, Biofuel, Ethanol, Hydrogen Fuel Cells, Nuclear Power, Off Shore Drilling, Alaskan Drilling, Gulf of Mexico Drilling, Oil from Coal, Oil from Shale, why not all of them?

The government should get out of the way and let it all happen. What the government was formed for and what it should continue to do is police the situation. Are the fuels safe? That is not a political question it is a police question. Is drilling safe? That is not a political question it is a police question. Are the fuel companies giving us the product that they are saying they are giving us? That is not a political question it is a police question.

None of this should be about price. Let the market take care of itself. Viagra, Levitra, Cialis, and the multitude of off brands that are marketed for men, cost a fortune. You can buy a bottle of sixty aspirins in the dollar store and you can buy one Viagra for ten to fifteen dollars a pill. How come? The market. Once the control is off the formula, the copycats will flood the market and the market and the market price will adjust. In the meantime the only thing that would adjust the market price would be a price war, or the market drying up because of the price. Even at the most recent high price of gasoline, you could still buy three gallons of gas for the price of one male enhancement pill.

No one wants dirty air, nor does anyone want others to foul up the ground or the water. The people who do foul up the ground, air and water generally do it for money. Not to make money but to save money. Treating their stack emissions, cleaning the toxins from the material that goes into the earth and the water is an expensive undertaking. Not doing it should be more expensive. The fines collected by the Earth and Atmosphere Police should be used solely for the purpose of funding the

Earth and Atmosphere Police and the clean up. Eluding the fines and the clean up cost would be the impetus for finding means to treat and clean the waste and turn the remnants into capital. For example; algae is a vegetable which can be crushed to extract oil. The oil can be converted to bio-fuel. Algae require carbon dioxide and water, preferably dirty water to grow. Dirty water contains nitrogen and algae grow faster with nitrogen. Therefore, if you grow algae using carbon dioxide you would be cleaning the air. And if you used water containing nitrogen and the algae took the nitrogen from the water, you would be cleaning the water. Then the bio-fuel created from the algae would burn cleaner with less emissions and the air would be further cleaned. The solution to many problems lies in getting at them. Perhaps the byproduct of cleaning the toxins from waste products could yield that substance which would make a male enhancement pill that can be purchased in the dollar store. Clean air and water and male enhancement pill, who could ask for more?

Business & Unions

We all know that in the late 1800s and early 1900s there were businesspeople who were unscrupulous. They took advantage of their workers and provided them with unfair wages and unsafe working conditions. Their motivation was profit and they made money on the backs of their employees. Technology was growing and the machines that were coming on line were not always safe. History is replete with scenarios of workers not being thought of as valued employees but an expendable commodity necessary to attain a goal. Bridge building and erection of skyscrapers were construction projects that cost many workers there lives.

Unions came into being in the early 1900s to meet a specific need. They were formed to provide a voice for the workers and give strength to the cause of bettering wages and working conditions. Initially it was a battleground on which many people suffered. But like most things in life, you can have too much of a good thing. Unions after a time began to serve their own ends.

When I was going through a Master's program, I did a paper on regional governments. One of the quotes that I used in my paper was that "bureaucracies, once formed, serve themselves." I'm not sure I have the words exactly right, and I don't remember who wrote it or said it before me, but the thought is correct. Unions are another form of a bureaucracy. Staying alive and functional becomes the main function of the union once it is formed. Every year or two when the contract must be renewed, the union has a meeting to determine what the demands of the union will be. Those demands are taken to the employer in an effort to formulate the new contract. Imagine if the union president stood before the members and said, "We did pretty good last year but this year we need to do better. I want you people to stop using so much sick time and stop being late. We need higher production and with that, we also need fewer mistakes, too many of the products we produce are being rejected for poor quality. For now I think that we should take fifty cents less an hour until we cure those problems." Would he or she ever be elected again? The president would probably impeached. The membership wants more, and when they have the power associated with being organized they can demand more.

My mother worked for a company called Atwater Kent in the early part of the 1900s just prior to the depression. She told me that the workers became unionized and when the union had gained sufficient strength amongst the workers, called on management to revise the contract. Management either refused to negotiate or refused the demands and the union went on strike. The strike took place in the autumn of the year. The autumn was the busiest time since much of the product line, which included radios and other electronics, were purchased as Christmas gifts. Mr. Atwater Kent (the person who owned the company) capitulated and when the workers came back to work he warned them that if they went on strike again he would close. They did and he did.

To some extent that same thing has been happening over an over again in the business community. Companies that close and move to other countries, or in some cases relocate in the United States to a place where unions are not strong, are escaping the power of the union. The companies sometimes move to better their bottom line, however some move for their survival.

The basic principle of business is to sell something for more than it costs you. Whether you build it yourself, grow it yourself or sell it yourself, the product must cost less to produce and get to the consumer than the consumer is willing to pay. If you are the only person involved in your business, your income will always be limited since your production is the sole element that determines how much money you can make. People begin to make more money when people work for them. Generally, the balance should be that a person working for you makes you more money than he or she costs you. When you have a lot of people working for you and you adhere to that principle, you should make a lot of money. There is a balance that must be struck when the worker becomes valuable to the success of your business. Generally, it is wise to pay the valuable person well and make them happy in their work so that they will continue to work for you. The other side of the coin is when a worker costs you more than he or she makes for you, you must get rid of the person as soon as possible to limit your loss. There are many other factors that make up the equation of an equitable wage, among which is the availability of trained workers, the potential to grow the market and hire more workers, the cost effectiveness of training, and supervising workers to increase the bottom line.

When the union comes into the picture all of the workers become equal. The good highly trained and motivated worker cannot make more than the poorly motivated worker. There can be variations in a piecework shop or union approved incentive based pay, but for the most part union workers are paid by their seniority and not by the quality of work they perform. A large company with stockholders must make public the income and expenses at the end of the year, and the union becomes aware of the profitability of the business. The union instills in the worker the feeling of unfairness when the company makes a nice profit off the backs of the workers. The workers continue to seek more and more until the company determines that it is the company's best interest to relocate to a place that is non-union. In Philadelphia in the 1940s and 1950s there were a number of knitting mills where large numbers of people were employed. From the union and the workers perspective, the employers who took their business south leaving no knitting mills in the Philadelphia area, were scoundrels who did not want to pay a fair wage. To the business owners who moved, they got out from under the stranglehold of the unions who were choking the profitability out of their company.

The truth lies, as usual, somewhere in the middle. There were unions who made demands that were unreasonable and when the company attempted to keep its profitability the union struck and shutdown the company. The earlier strikes led to a great deal of violence, but by the

1960s there were few people who were willing to try to stand up to the unions by force. Some of the workers who could not afford to be on strike and tried to work during the strike for their employer were sometimes injured or worse. During the 1960s and early 1970s most violence that occurred in the area that I worked in the Police Department was instigated by the union. Some companies continued after the strike but some were forced to evaluate the cost of relocation against the cost of labor and they chose the former. Of course, there were business owners who had profitable businesses and many loyal employees upon whom the business owner relied. And yet they still sought the increased measure of profitability from cheaper labor. They closed and moved away leaving the workers with no jobs and no futures. To some extent each of the parties, the business owner and the unionized employees, created the negative approach that the other party had toward the working environment. The worker would think, the owner is only in it for the money, doesn't care about me, so why should I break my back just so he (or they) can have a new Mercedes or a bigger home in suburbs. The business owner would think, they (the workers) don't care that I put my life's savings into this business and if it fails I am in the waste pit. They (the workers) don't care about the quality of the product or the profitability of the business, they just want a paycheck that grows every year and a benefit package that costs a fortune.

Common sense would tell us that the message or feelings of the parties must be amended. Each side should understand that the success of the business is an integral part of their own success and happiness. Many things that could improve a product or the profitability of a company are thought of by the employees at any level of the business. The climate should be right for those improvements to be sought by both sides. Part of the improved profitability of a business rests on the safety and welfare of the employees. Unlike the early 1900s, when you became sick or injured as a result of a work related matter, you were out of work. Today, the expense of such a circumstance can be huge to the employer. The insurance premium for the policy that covers the employee is usually based upon the previous claims. Therefore, if an employee can find a safer way to perform a task or eliminate a health hazard, the employer saves a great deal of money as well as not losing employees to injury or illness. Employers and employees should communicate openly and honestly. Perhaps the time has come for the union to adapt to a new type of representation that is more interested in the profitability of the business that hire their members and not the survival of their bureaucracy. Any employer who did not welcome an open dialogue with the employee's representative would be a fool.

There is no easy answer to the issue of unions and business, but as the union membership declines one must wonder who to blame for the exodus of labor intensive business from the U.S. When you begin the examination, you must also include the government. Government employees are allowed to unionize now. Governments cannot close up and move away to avoid the higher wages demanded by unions, but they need not worry about profitability. Government is in the unique position of being able to charge whatever they want for the product they deliver and, as consumers, the only thing that we can do is move away. As long as we stay in the community served by the government in question we have to pay the taxes.

What this has caused is a skewing of wages and benefits in the favor of the union workers who are employed by the government. When I joined the Police Department in the early 1960s the common wisdom was that a government job didn't pay all that much, but it was secure. You would always get paid, you had decent benefits and when you retired you would get an insured pension. Today it seems that among working people a job in the government is a homerun.

The government in the form of Ronald Reagan dealt a blow to the unions when he terminated all of the air traffic controllers. In my humble opinion they deserved it. There are things that for the benefit of all of the country (the populace) must be allowed to operate without interruption. The Police and Fire Departments are two of those things. The armed forces of the United States are also in the same class. Air traffic is now the life blood of commerce in our country. Many things of great importance are transported by air aside from passengers. Some of the travel of passengers is necessary for the health and safety of all of us. Clearly, at the time, the strike of air traffic controllers could not be abided.

I happened to be working at the time and was a police supervisor on the picket line at the Philadelphia International Airport. I had a discussion with one of the strikers and found that he made considerably more than a Captain in the Police Force. His main complaint concerning why he needed more money was to be compensated for the stress of his position. He worked in a tower that was air conditioned in the summer and heated in the winter. He got periodic breaks from his position, regular mealtimes and could relieve himself whenever necessary. He said the stress came from having so many lives depend on the actions of the air traffic controller. The young man was in his early thirties, and he complained of having a bad stomach from the stress. However, upon recognizing the size of his stomach and questioning him concerning his diet, I couldn't be certain of the reason for his bad digestive system.

All of that aside, the government is in part responsible for the strength and perhaps the demise of the labor unions. The Democratic Party has long been the party of organized labor. Many of the big cities are Democratic strongholds and most of them have passed legislation to allow only union workers on government contract jobs. Some jobs are closed shop jobs in that they require new employees to join the union after an initial introductory period. The unions have been able to get away with many things that would otherwise be criminal, such as overcharging union members for benefits and membership and by siphoning off funds that were to have been earmarked for other things. But mostly the government has ignored the connection of unions and organized crime. Unions have always given large donations to the candidates who support their cause and the politicians who receive the contributions repay the donations with contracts for huge amounts of government funds. Both the donations and the fat contracts are the result of workers money, whether as union dues or taxes.

Republicans have long been the supporters of business and business the supporter of Republicans. Republicans legislate tax breaks and subsidies as well as preferential treatment for businesses that are the financial supporters of the Party. The money paid to them from the government coffers is tax money and the money given to the Republicans also has to be looked at as tax money.

In both cases without an agreement for quid pro quo there would be no contributions and there would be no favorable contracts or subsidies, which leaves the non-union shop at a distinct disadvantage when trying to bid a job in a climate where the bid is rigged. The business that doesn't play the game is at a competitive disadvantage to the business receiving tax breaks and incentives to enhance the friendly business's bottom line. The parties to this arrangement make too much money and have too comfortable an existence to change anything.

For the most part, however, small private enterprise businesses and worker arrangements work just fine. The capitalistic systems controls the marketplace and the business. When you are sharp at what you do and put together something that people either want or need they will come to you. Workers who are treated properly and paid a wage commensurate with the quality of their work are anxious to provide good service to the employer. Both parties are overwhelmingly interested in the health of the business and its continuity. It is the large and competitive marketplace that the entry of the government into the picture makes the field uneven. The motivation behind government subsidies remains a mystery to the everyday person and voter. But to those in the field, subsidies can make a business extremely profitable.

The government should only subsidize new businesses that are providing a much needed service or product to the entire population or will benefit the entire population. Subsidies should be published for all to see and the sponsor and the recipient should also be made public. If the general public is helping to pay for a product or service through their tax dollars, they should not be gouged for a huge profit at the other end. This type of support stifles the spirit of capitalist enterprise. Why would someone want to make a better product cheaper when they are making a fortune by collecting from the consumer for manufacturing (by a tax endowed subsidy) and again when the product is sold?

THE LATEST ECONOMIC CRISIS

As I write this material we in the United States and to some degree the entire world are in the throes of an economic crisis. My theory of this crisis is that it was brought about by all or most of the things I have already stated in this book, greed and other evil motivation as well as a total lack of common sense.

Let us start with the everyday person. Joe Average is in the market for a new home. He has lived in his home for many years and during that time the value of the property went up. But now there has been a sudden acceleration in the value of the property. Joe suddenly feels quite rich. Is he? With a rare exception, no. Why not? Well simply because the price of Joe's house is also the price of every home in the area of like size and shape. Joe has to move somewhere else and the price of that house has increased just like Joe's. Therefore, with rare exception, everyone who sells their home at the increased value will pay an increased value for the next home. Well then, who is profiting from the increased value. The list is long and you aren't on it.

First, when Joe sells his home the real estate commission will be commensurate with the price of the house so the agent will make more money. Second, the government will take in more tax dollars whether the house is sold or not because the assessment goes up and the real estate and school taxes go up with it. Third, once the sale is made, the mortgage broker will make points. A point is one percent of the mortgage amount. In most cases that I have seen, the lender must pay three points for the placement of the mortgage. That means that the loan placement or whatever the points are described as will cost the borrower $3,000 per one hundred thousand dollars of mortgage amount. Fourth, the title insurance policy is based upon the price and would increase as the price of the home increases. Fifth, the government also has a tax called the transfer tax. Sometimes it is paid to the local government and sometimes to state government. Sometimes it is paid to both. It is generally a percent or two, but in Philadelphia it is four percent. So if the house value went from seventy-five thousand to one hundred seventy-five thousand, the transfer tax is increased by four thousand dollars in Philadelphia. And then there is capital gains.

As I see it, the only beneficiary other than the ones already shown is the rare person with more than one house. They decide to sell one and not replace it. Then just like the profit on a stock, the increased value of your home is taxable to the I.R.S. Capital gains is, as I stated earlier, an alleged gain. What I mean by that is when you bought the house, what was the property worth as compared to a loaf of bread, a quart of milk or a gallon of gasoline? In 1963 I bought a brand new Dodge Lancer. The cost was just over two thousand dollars. I was used to no accessories, so I did not include a radio, just a heater. It did have turning signals however. No more did I have to roll down the window in the cold or rain to shove my arm out to signal that I was making a left turn, or angle my hand over the roof to indicate a right turn. Today, I would guess that a car of like size, power and comfort would cost between fifteen and twenty thousand, so let's say ten times more money. (It is hard to compare because while the Lancer was a midsize it was the larger than a lot of cars on the road today. Furthermore, the additional accessories today are all standard. The motor was a powerful six cylinder and the cars of like size are all four cylinders)

I bought a house in 1964 which cost close to eleven thousand. It was slightly below average because the house needed repair and I was handy. By my calculation, if I lived in that house today and sold it, the house would sell for ten times what I paid. Somewhere between one hundred thousand and one hundred twenty thousand would be the equivalent of what I paid. So would I have made a one hundred or more thousand dollar profit? Not likely. Make the comparison to the everyday cost of other things. Some prices have gone up more and some less, but the return on the house if converted to bread, milk or gasoline would probably represent the same buying power. Again, where is the gain? Why should the government be entitled to a portion of the value of my home which in buying power and almost every other comparison has remained the same.

The next part of the crisis came when Joe Average became greedy. Joe saw the rapidly climbing house values and felt that they would continue to climb. Joe began to look at homes that were beyond his means, thinking that in a few years the value would continue to rise and if the mortgage payment became burdensome, he would sell with no trouble for a much higher price and walk away with a nice nest egg. Joe was better off than some, because he did have some part of a nest egg from the house he sold.

Jack Not-So-Average, on the other hand, did not have a house to sell. He had no nest egg on which to rely for a down payment and didn't make enough to afford the mortgage payment on the house next door to Joe's. However, he, like everyone else saw the market price of homes catapulting into the stratosphere and wanted in on the easy money. Jack went to one of the other people making a lot of money from the increase in home values, the mortgage broker, and sought help. The broker, always wanting to help anyone get a mortgage whether there was any true hope they would pay it off or not, was able to place Jack in a no-doc mortgage. (No doc means no documentation) The fiction concerning the increase in home values and the belief that it would continue unabated gave the broker the solace that was necessary to make the lender and Jack believe that this was an OK deal. Jack had his choice of an interest only mortgage for the first five years (meaning he paid nothing toward the principal) or an ARM (adjustable rate mortgage) wherein, for the first five years the payments are low and then the payments catapult through the roof, based on an equation that includes the prime rate and a nice profit for the mortgage company. Both were bad, but I think the ARM was worse. The broker was either unscrupulous or stupid. The thought that the rising home prices would never reach a ceiling was stupid. If the broker knew that the cap would be reached sometime, sooner or later, he was unscrupulous. The brokers got their fee at the settlement table and had nothing to do with Jack or the mortgage company after that. Both Jack and the mortgage company are now mired in debt.

The failure of Jack and the mortgage company is the prime reason for our economic crisis. Greed overcame common sense. If these were not government inspired mortgages, none of this would have ever happened. Prior to government's intervention in the mortgage arena, if you walked into a bank and asked for a loan you would have provided enough information to the bank officer to feel that he/she would soon be counting the pairs of underwear in your drawer before you'd get a loan. The bank has people to answer to and therefore exhibit great care in making loans. The main interest of a private lender is the ability for the borrower to payback the loan with interest. The bank has no interest in advancing social causes or in making a profit off of submitting loans for approval. The bank only makes money from interest. The government on the other hand tries to use taxpayer's dollars to advance causes of importance to them. Many of the causes and the proposed solutions advance the aims of a small number of people within the government. For the most part the hidden aim is the advancement or security of the small number of people. Like many other things undertaken by the government, the Fannie and Freddie endeavor is a failure that will cost us a fortune in taxpayer dollars. The aim was to probably advance homeownership to people who could not otherwise afford to buy a home, but ended with being mismanaged and allowing profit-taking by unscrupulous mortgage brokers. The availability of mortgages to those who would not otherwise qualify was probably a huge factor in the seller's market in real estate and to some extent explains the rapid increase a few years ago in the price of real estate. No one wanted to look beyond the surface and see that it couldn't sustain itself. The market was out of whack because the marketplace was altered by conditions outside of the market.

Government seems to never learn that the marketplace should rule the marketplace. When the price of a commodity is not controlled by the true demand, the market is doomed to failure. Just as consumption controls need, need controls demand and demand controls price. Subsidies and other outside adjustments cause the market to lose its balance and skitter off the path. Not a good thing. Politicians, keep your hands out of the pie.

IMMIGRATION AND FOREIGN AID

The first question you might ask is, "Why are the two things placed together?" Well, I think that foreign aid has a great deal to do with immigration. Certainly, if someone watched the news from America they would not feel that it was a very safe place. Admittedly, there are countries that have problems regarding the safety of its citizens, but if the consideration were citizen on citizen crime, we seem to lead the world statistically. So, the decision to emigrate to America would not be based on personal safety. I think it is based on economy. The people who wish to come to America feel that they will have better economic opportunity. I think that the feeling of more opportunity comes from American movies shown in foreign countries and the knowledge of foreign aid. We are a country with so much money that we give it away to other countries. With that kind of wealth, there must be enough around for the person considering emigration to make a decent living.

Did you ever wonder why we have to give foreign aid? I have. The obvious reason would be charity. We are coming to the aid of those less fortunate than ourselves. There is no proof that that is what is actually happening though. We do send aid when a disaster strikes, but that would be an unscheduled distribution of funds. One of the regularly scheduled distributions has been reportedly going to Pakistan, our ally. The amount is billions. I have never seen an accounting of the billions we send to Pakistan. For example, How much was spent on food, construction, given to the needy, etc.? Has the money been spent to build infrastructure, like clean water or sewage systems? We never know. My own opinion is that we are throwing money down a rat hole.

We are like the rich kid who goes into a poor neighborhood and treats the kids to ice cream in an attempt to buy a few friends. I think that Musharif was creating a nice 401K on our cash. Certainly there are some good things. An example might be if the government purchased American products which would help farmers in a foreign country produce more and better crops and provided this equipment to that country. There would be a double benefit. However, we don't get much information about it. I think the reason that we don't get information about foreign aid is because the people responsible for giving away our tax dollars either can't give an explanation for where it goes or they would be embarrassed by the explanation. We should ask. We should keep on asking until we are told.

Immigration is as inexplicable as foreign aid. In the Philadelphia area there are many different stories to the immigration issue. When I was a child, the neighborhoods in Philadelphia were broken up along ethnic and racial lines. There seemed to be a grouping of Italians in South Philadelphia. However, in the eastern section of South Philadelphia there was an Irish enclave. Polish people seemed to group together in Bridesburg (another section of Philadelphia) and Jewish people lived in Oxford Circle and the northern section of West Oak Lane. There were Germans in the Olney section. But for a rare disagreement across the imaginary boundary of the neighborhoods, this living arrangement allowed people to maintain an identity with their native country as well as feel a form of camaraderie with others. Stores located in those sections proudly spoke the native tongue to their customers if and when it was appropriate. I left out Chinatown (the residents were obviously Asian) and North Philadelphia where there was a concentration of African Americans. In both of these communities, the lines were more strictly drawn and the isolation from the surrounding communities more apparent.

Over time the lines were not as distinct. Today, the enclaves of ethnicity are almost gone. However, there are a few new groups in Philadelphia. The Northeast section has a Russian Jewish community as well a Brazilian and Asian influence. The issue about legal and illegal immigration is not as relevant in Philadelphia as it is in Laredo, but we are cognizant of the circumstances.

I have met many people in the Asian community and as a general rule I find them to be hardworking and self-reliant. They have a strong sense of community. They keep to themselves when they socialize to a large extent. However, the younger generation is not so inclined. I am aware of the difficulty that Asians experience when they try to sponsor someone from their native country to come to America. I am sure there are some illegal Asian immigrants in our country just as there are many illegal Brazilians and other South Americans.

What do we do concerning this problem? Well, first we should examine the problem. The first unfairness about this problem is that the illegal walks in to our country and takes root when and where he or she wants. The legal immigrant may wait years (in some cases 6 to 7 years) for the nod from the U.S. Government to legally come to our shores. Illegal immigrants work but pay no taxes. Legal immigrants work and pay taxes. The children of illegal immigrants go to our schools and both the children who in some cases are citizens (having been born here) and the parents avail themselves of social services. The legal immigrant has a sponsor who is supposed to insure that the immigrant does not become a burden to society.

That there is even an issue regarding what we should do about people in our country illegally is a statement of the problem with America today. Many feel that we must carefully address the situation because there are so many illegals in the country it is hard to enforce the law. This is more a political recognition of the power of the voting bloc of the Spanish community. In some communities police officers are not allowed to ask a person if they are in the country legally. There have been estimates that range from 10 million to 20 million people in our country illegally. I am not really aware of the total number of people who use illegal drugs or who use drugs illegally, but I would venture a guess that the number far exceeds 20 million, and we do still arrest them when it is brought to the attention of the authorities.

We usually cannot get any answers of quality from our political leaders because they don't want to do anything but put the blame on the opposing political party. When some street thug murders another person with a gun, politicians rail against the gun laws that allow street thugs to obtain guns. Having been a police officer, I am aware that it is against the law to carry an unlicensed gun on the streets of Philadelphia. Perhaps if the person with the gun was stopped by the police and frisked, the gun would have been found and the person arrested. If the gun was stolen or otherwise illegally obtained, the charges would be increased. We don't have to stop and frisk everyone. We have the capability of determining who is committing the murders by gun and pretty much it is males in the teenage to late twenties range. However, woe is the police officer who profiles based on age, race or sex to attempt to enforce the law with efficiency. Politicians are afraid to endorse a policy that would recognize statistical significance of race, age, sex or even legal status in the U.S. in the area of crime, cost of services, and other factors which negatively affect our quality of life. Any issue which would recognize statistical significance of criminal behavior amongst African American youths would be labeled racist by the African American community. Truth be told, the outcry would not be from people who were likely victims of crime, which would be African Americans who live in the lawless areas and could speak with anonymity.

What's the point? Laws must be enforced or removed from the code of laws. To do otherwise is to diminish the stature of laws as a guiding principle of our nation. To admit that there are twenty million people illegally in the U.S. is tantamount to saying we are a country without enforceable laws. Excusing the failure of our government to secure our borders based on a theory that we all want Mexicans in our country to do the jobs that we don't want to do is absurd. First of all, that is very demeaning to Mexicans. No one ever put the question to a vote. There are ways to become a guest worker in U.S. There are also means by which one can bring in workers when no workers can be found in the U.S. to do a specific task.

I have talked to people who use Mexicans as laborers and they uniformly respond that they are far superior workers to any non-Mexican that can be found to do the tasks required by a specific job. In the main it is because they show up for work on time and show up every day that they are required. Then, while they work, they don't stop for every cockamamie reason under the sun, but work continuously through the day. The Mexicans also appreciate the equipment they use and keep it in working order and make every effort not to damage the equipment. Basically, they seem to be happy with their employment and their job. They are not resentful (at least not openly) that the owner of the company or the boss is making money off of their labor. All of that said, I still do not agree with the wink and nod policy. The people who hire illegals don't do it because they are better workers, they do it because they are cheap labor. They work hard and create no trouble because they are illegal and are fearful of being brought to the attention of authorities.

In any event, the opinion of this writer is that we should either close our borders and enforce the closure, or just tell the world they can come and go as they please. Secondly, when a person comes to the attention of the authorities, proof should be demanded that would include identification that would allow a determination of legal status. Those in the country illegally should be sent back. As to the children of the illegal immigrant, the answer is more difficult. On the one hand the child has not done anything wrong and should therefore not be punished. On the other hand, the theory of tainted evidence might be applicable. When a search has been deemed to be illegal, all of the evidence found during that search is excluded from evidence as fruit from the poisoned tree. Using that logic on the immigration issue, the results of criminal behavior should not create positive legal standing. Therefore, children born to parents who are illegally in the country should not be granted citizenship. In support of that conclusion, it would ease the manner of deportation if the children of the illegal were sent with the deportee and their status as American citizens did not create the need for appointing counsel to protect their rights. It sounds a tad harsh, but so does deporting the parents and leaving the child in the care of strangers.

In summary, we should close the borders to undocumented visitors, and deport visitors who are here without legal status. We should demand a reasonable explanation for the huge sums of money that are given to foreign countries for aid. Secondary to that issue we should also have a clear understanding of why it is correct behavior to give large sums of money to people who don't like us.

WHAT'S RIGHT WITH US, U.S.

W hen I read letters to the editorial page written by regular citizens, I am heartened by what is right. Despite the fact that many of the letters are in drastic disagreement with my position on various subjects, I am still thankful that people take the time to write and have the courage of their convictions. Some people trumpet the words of the news media or some misguided politician or political party, but they had to have read the words or listened to the news report to form their opinion. It is that fact that causes me to be heartened. They are interested. I listen to talk radio and hear the same thing, people willing to state their opinions for broadcast over the airwaves.

Most of the people who speak or write, aside from the professionals, are of good heart and mind and believe that their position has merit. That is not to say that they don't have an ulterior motive for their position. Some people like the Democratic party because they think that the party is pro working person and since they fit that bill, the party will be good for them. Conversely, some people like the Republican party because it is portrayed as being favorable to business and the wealthy, and they are either in business or wealthy or hope to be and therefore see the party as promoting their interest.

There are also one issue people. Abortion, gun rights, immigration, and like subjects could be the sole interest of the person. While we could say that that person doesn't see the whole picture, how many of us actually see the whole picture? People with one issue are usually more well informed on that issue than those of us who look in broader terms at life and the good of the U.S. Abortion for example is a subject that defies an easy answer. Is the world over-populated? Certainly. Is abortion the answer to controlling the population? Not likely. Is the killing of an infant in the birth canal the right thing to do? Not if I had to watch it. Is it right to force a woman who was gang raped by a pack of Neanderthals to give birth to child of that rape? Not in my world. Do I have the answer? No. Some people think they do and support their positions with sound arguments. The other side of the issue also can give sound arguments in support of their opposition. That is wholesome debate. Provided that debate doesn't get out of hand, it is healthy to explore the various sides of an issue. We should all be grateful that in the U.S. we are able to state our position without fear of reprisal.

During this latest election cycle there seems to be no place that you can go in public without hearing something election related. We are blessed with the freedom of our opinions. But more important than politics, we are blessed with many people of honest wholesome motivation. Police, fire-fighters, little league coaches, teachers, and regular people who are invested with a desire to make the world a better place.

I earlier spoke of the change in the U.S. and the world during my lifetime. Many of the changes came as a result of the efforts of people in the U.S. My uncle was one of those people. I told his story in the first chapter and will repeat it here because it typifies what is great about our country. My father's brother was a guy who was not such a great student in his youth. I don't believe that he finished high school. He was born prior to 1910 and passed away in his early sixties. During his life he was captivated by electronics. In the early part of his life he made crystal radios. He was able, somehow, to be recognized for his talent and was hired by Philco and worked in the lab. When I was teenager in the 1950s, I would go to his home in Glenside and be wowed by the equipment that he had in his basement. Many of his co-employees would visit his home over the weekend. That was also the most likely time for my family to visit. I met men with master's degrees and doctorates in fields related to electronics. They came to my uncle's home to work with him on projects. All of them held my uncle in the highest of esteem.

These were the people who worked on microphones and stereos and obtained for Philco a number of patents that helped Philco remain profitable during that time period. My uncle regaled me with music from a stereo that he had created for his own use at home, and I was in awe. It was the first time that I was able to hear an orchestra play music and hear the various instruments come from different speakers around the room as though I was sitting in the orchestra pit dead center. He and his associates worked with different materials that were used inside of the speakers that looked like tin foil and was what expanded the range of speakers to what we now take for granted.

The spirit of those years is still alive and well. There are many people today who have the desire to improve on everything they see. To some, their efforts do not seem significant, because they may be streamlining an administrative process to save time and money. Others may be finding a way to speed up service on our internet. We have come to a point where we expect that the electronics item we purchased today will be obsolete by the time we get it home and out of the box. My uncle described the computer that he worked on (developed) at work. The computer took up a large room. It was on a raised floor to allow for air circulation in an attempt to keep the computer cool as it was believed that the computer must remain at a constant 72 degrees. He and his associates were working on a type of magnetic tape as a source for maintaining the memory of the computer. The computer at his work was experimental and cost a fortune in parts and labor, but couldn't hold a candle to the one I am typing on right now. This computer was purchased brand new in around 1998 for about eight hundred dollars. I like to say that it has more memory than the defense department. Suffice to say electronically we have come a long way in the last fifty years. Automobiles, household appliances, garden tools, power tools, and a list too long to put here of items that are far better than anything available in the 1950s.

What is responsible for these improvements? There is only one answer. It is capitalism. A shampoo which cleans your scalp and your hair and leaves it feeling lustrous instead of frizzed can make money for the company that invents it. It can be a source of wealth and pride to the people responsible for the formula. You never hear the word homogenized today, but when I was growing up milk was pasteurized and homogenized. That meant it was safe to drink and the homogenization mixed the cream and the skim milk to the product we simply call milk. Prior to homogenization, the cream rested on top of the milk and you shook it to mix it when you used it. Someone developed that process and made milk more saleable because of the change in the product. Milk use to come in glass and had a paper or cardboard cap. You had to carry the milk carefully as the caps were not as sealed as the containers we use today. These items have all made the product better and more saleable. There are many people in our world today, especially in our country working to better a product or make a new product that is better than what we used in the past.

Sometimes those people bring about bad things when they make something good. The bad things were mechanization that removed the need for workers. Bad things were automobiles that put blacksmiths and wagon makers out of business. Also bad was automation and computers which took many workers from the lines in factories and replaced them with robotic arms and mechanization. Jack hammers replaced men with sledge hammers. Front loader-back hoes replaced ditch diggers. The list is endless. But bad is in the eye of the beholder. Progress leaves some behind. With the speed of progress today we should train our citizens from an early age to be aware of progress. Plan for it and be a part of it.

The good thing is that we have been able to mass produce and when you look back it is hard to remember the time when there weren't televisions in every room. It is hard to remember having a hard line phone in the house, and it was the only phone for the entire family. It is hard to remember the family car as the only car in the family. Before that there was a time when Uncle Jake was the only person we knew with a car and he would come and take us for a ride on Sunday. It is hard to remember the little battery operated portable radio with the three foot antennae that still couldn't pick up music or the ballgame unless it was aimed just perfectly. But we have survived and very nicely

I might add. We can all find something to complain about. Automation was at one time the enemy. In the auto industry, automation has made cars more efficient, and safer and able to last a great deal longer than earlier vehicles. How could we live without air conditioning? When I grew up we were lucky to have an electric fan.

Where did all of the innovation come from that has transported products from South America, Europe, Asia and all other spots on the globe to our doorstep for our use and eating pleasure? It came from the inventive nature of the citizens of the U.S. to a large measure and the willingness of the capitalistic system to embrace new products and new systems for bringing new products to the consumers of the U.S. In the 1950s I was in the Navy and went to Europe on a cruise. On the way home from the cruise, I couldn't wait to get back to the U.S. for a chocolate chip cookie and some cold cow's milk. I went to Poland in the 1970s and found that people could wait in a long line to go into a grocery store that was much less than fully stocked with meat and fresh fruit and all of the items that we take for granted. This is undoubtedly the greatest nation in the world in which to live.

Sure we have crime problems, teenage pregnancy problems, high school drop-out problems, unemployment problems, but mostly we have a total lack of common sense problem. We absolutely refuse to look at the foregoing problems and many other things in a common sense fashion. Our forefathers had common sense. Someday take a look at the documents that formed our nation and you will be shocked to see how simple they are. If Washington, Jefferson, Hamilton and Franklin were to set eyes on our tax code, they would set sail back to England. But their framework is still here and the American spirit is still here. We are the same people who shocked the world during the Second World War with our ability to get behind the effort and produce war implements that saved the world from domination by a fascist. We can do this. How you might ask?

Simply by taking a deeper look. Take an interest in something, not necessarily everything. When your children are young take an interest in schools and related issues. When the kids are grown take an interest in local government. Read the newspaper instead of simply accepting the news reporters on television. In my law practice I warned people who were going into partnerships business and personal, to enter as though your partner was your enemy. Set down the rules for each other as though the person was going to take advantage at every turn. When you started out that way you could probably remain friends. If you simply entered as friends it was almost a certainty you would end up enemies. Approach the news reporter, the politician, the teacher, the person with an opinion that wants to tell you what it is, with skepticism. Examine their motivation and your own. It is easy to say you want good government, but it is harder to work toward getting it. We have become divorced from the life around us because we are too interested in our own important things. However, when we look back at all of those time consuming important things later in life they don't seem so important. In a church sermon, the pastor was speaking to material wealth when he said that he had been in the company of many people who were passing to the next life and never heard one of them say that they would die happy if they had only owned one more Lexus. He heard many say that they should have spent more time with their family.

There is nothing mystical about our opinions and our desires. They come from within our own brain. Unfortunately, we don't stand guard at our brain to determine the information going in. If we did we would bar a great many things from entry. There is a phrase used in business and educational settings regarding the processing of information and it is "garbage in, garbage out." In other words, the output of our brains can only be as good as the information that is put into it. When I was a child, my brain told me that I did not like vegetables. Something happened to the flow of information into my brain during my lifetime, because I now thoroughly enjoy what used to make me gag. Broccoli, cauliflower, peppers, string beans, beets, and many more are welcome to my plate and my palate. What happened? I'd like to explain it this way. I asked my brain what it was that made it react to peas and lima beans in that way when in fact they were both good for me and would help me remain healthy. The answers, which I had to search for, were that the other children I observed eating vegetables when I was a child made faces indicating their dislike and my parents treated vegetables as something that had to be eaten for some reason, which did not include taste. Subsequently, I formed the opinion that I did not like vegetables.

Many of our beliefs are formed in the same way. Unfiltered information is allowed into our brain and gets to alter or out rightly make our opinions. No one would ever question the veracity of Walter Cronkite, but wasn't he just reading a script. Not to discredit Walter, because he very well might have written his own script. But if we look at someone and think nice thoughts about them, we give them credibility they might not deserve. If we ask directions of a gorgeous woman or a handsome man, we follow them almost without question because we want them to be right and we want to agree with someone who is so good-looking. Well you see, that is just the information we should question. Why? Because no one else is questioning the information and that good-looking person gets the feeling that they can't be wrong. Important issues such as our health and therefore what we eat should not be left to untested and unverified opinions of another. Nor should we vote for a candidate without knowing why. Go beyond the looks, and the promises, which almost never come to pass, to the things which are important. Character, personal history, judgment can all be determined by looking to the resume. What has the person accomplished and what have they failed to accomplish. Tell your brain what it should think by controlling the information that your brain keeps. You can't stop things from going in, but you can control what is there when you need to make a decision. Be apart of what makes this country great by starting to believe that it is great and you will find many things to support your view.

Just do it.